There Leviathan,
Hugest of living creatures in the deep
Stretched like a promontory sleeps or swims,
And seems a moving land; and at his gills
Draws in, and at his breath spouts out a sea.

—Milton, *Paradise Lost*

THE *Spirit* OF THE WHALE

LEGEND, HISTORY, CONSERVATION

Jane Billinghurst, Editor

VOYAGEUR PRESS

DEDICATION

To my research assistants, Olivia and Edward Patton

ACKNOWLEDGMENTS

Thank you to my husband, Tom, and my daughters, Stephanie and Nicola, who accompanied me on many of my trips while I researched this book. Your patience is appreciated. Thank you to Michael Dregni at Voyageur Press for suggesting that I undertake this project, to Amy Rost-Holtz for her helpful and encouraging editing, and to Dr. Phil Clapham for his expert comments on whale biology. Any errors of fact or interpretation that remain are mine.

Edited by Amy Rost-Holtz
Designed by Kristy Tucker

Printed in Hong Kong

00   01   02   03   04   5   4   3   2   1

Library of Congress Cataloging-in-Publication Data

The spirit of the whale : legend, history, conservation / Jane
    Billinghurst, editor.
        p.   cm.
    Includes bibliographical references.
    ISBN 0-89658-409-7
    1. Whales. 2. Human-animal relationships. I. Billinghurst,
Jane, 1958–   .
QL737.C4S65 2000
599.5—dc21   99-40265
                    CIP

Published by Voyageur Press, Inc.
123 North Second Street, P.O. Box 338, Stillwater, MN 55082 U.S.A.
651-430-2210, fax 651-430-2211

Educators, fundraisers, premium and gift buyers, publicists, and marketing managers: Looking for creative products and new sales ideas? Voyageur Press books are available at special discounts when purchased in quantities, and special editions can be created to your specifications. For details contact the marketing department at 800-888-9653.

Page 1: *Photograph © Ron LeValley/Larry Ulrich Stock Photography*
Pages 2–3: *"Suddenly a mighty mass emerged from the water, and shot up perpendicularly into the air. It was the whale."*
—*Joseph C. Hart,* Miriam Coffin or the Whale Fisherman *(1834) (Photograph © John Hyde, Wild Things Photography)*
Page 3: *A humpback whale striking the water with its tail in an action known as lob-tailing. (Photograph © Tom Walker)*

CONTENTS

INTRODUCTION

Sunglare and sea pale as tears.
One long hour we watched the black whales
circling like dancers,
sliding dark backs out of water,
waving their heaved tails,
about an eyepupil-round spot
just a knife-edge
this side of the horizon.

Black whales, let me join in your dance
uncumbered by ego, my soul well anchored
in a brain bigger than I am
. . . multiplied tons of muscled flesh
roaring in organized tones of thunder
for kilometres. When I love
let me love gigantically; and when I dance
let the earth take note
as the sea takes note of you.

—Milton Acorn, "Whale Poem"

More than 70 percent of the earth's surface is covered by the ocean. In this watery realm live creatures whose size is almost inconceivable to those of us who live on land. Blue whales are the largest creatures ever to have lived on this planet; measured by mass, they are larger even than the largest dinosaurs. Sperm whales have the largest brains of any animal—five to six times the size of ours. Since the first coastal peoples encountered whales, we have struggled to define our relationship with these enormous creatures. We have revered them, we have destroyed them, and finally, it seems, we are seeking to understand them.

For many coastal peoples, whales have always been symbols of power in a world that transcends human interests and understanding. To early European sailors who came upon whales in the oceans by chance, they were monsters with fearsome powers of destruction; to land dwellers who found their carcasses washed up on beaches, they were objects of curiosity.

In A.D. 1100, the Basque people of northern Spain moved from chance encounters with whales to hunting them for commercial gain. Like Aboriginal peoples before them, they discovered that despite its enormous size, a whale can be caught by a hunter in a small boat armed with nothing more than a hand-held harpoon and enough rope to play out after the whale as it tried to escape. Aboriginal peoples depended on whales for their survival; to

A humpback whale flukes up before a dive. Humpbacks are notoriously exuberant whales. Nineteenth-century author and seaman Frank Bullen was of the opinion that "there be few creatures in earth, air, or sea that lead a happier life, or enjoy it with a greater zest than the humpback." (Photograph © John Hyde, Wild Things Photography)

twelfth-century Europeans, whales became a commercial resource to be exploited. The whalers did not understand that the supply of whales was limited. As one whaling ground after another was fished out, they assumed there were more whales to be had in other parts of the world.

The destruction of whale stocks around the world was systematic. Before the discovery of petroleum or the invention of plastic right and bowhead whales in the Atlantic, sperms whales deep in oceans around the world, gray whales along the California coast, and humpback whales migrating off the coasts of Africa and Australia were heavily pursued. From these hunts, markets were supplied with whale oil for cooking, lighting, and lubrication, and with whalebone (baleen) for women's fashions and household items that required a strong, flexible material.

At the end of the nineteenth century, just as substitutes were being found for whale oil and women's fashions were moving to styles no longer dependent on the firm yet flexible support provided by whale-bone, the technology of nautical hunting took a great leap forward to ensure that whaling did not become obsolete. The exploding harpoon gun and the factory ship brought the swift and massive rorquals of the Antarctic—blues, fins, and seis—within the whalers' purview; whale products were once again competitive in world markets—this time in the form of soap, margarine, and pet food.

By the 1930s, the firm conviction that God had put whales into the oceans to be exploited by humans was beginning to be assailed by a nagging doubt about the sustainability of whaling. It was obvious that the whaling industry was going to be in trouble if there were no more whales to hunt. No longer were whales viewed as an inexhaustible natural resource; they were viewed as a resource to be managed for the maximum benefit of commercial interests.

From the 1930s to the 1960s, whaling nations attempted to intro-duce hunting restrictions that would ensure a supply of whales for the whalers of the future. One of the main obstacles to achieving this supply, however, was that the oceans were common ground for all nations, and the laudable ideal of long-term cooperation for the greater good was offset by the pressing reality of immediate competition for limited resources. As a result whale quotas were set impossibly high, and the destruction of whales continued apace. The crisis, however, did begin systematic scientific research on the animals, as whaling interests decided to find out more about whales—dead whales, that is—in order to more efficiently exploit those that still roamed the ocean.

By the 1970s it seemed sustainable whaling might not be a practical idea after all. The emphasis began to change from managing whale stocks for commercial exploitation to saving whale stocks, period. As the possibility loomed that there might one day be oceans without whales, questions began to be raised about what this would mean. The concerns ranged from possible disastrous changes in climate and fish stocks to aesthetic concerns about the impoverishment of life in a world from which these huge creatures had been eliminated.

On January 1, 1986, a global moratorium on commercial whaling came into effect, and most research, with the exception of a limited

Right whales were the "right" whales for whalers to kill. They were fat and slow-moving, but best of all they floated when dead. (Photograph © Jeff Foott)

catch for scientific purposes, moved from the examination of whale carcasses aboard factory ships to the observation of live whales in the oceans. No longer was the relationship between people and whales to be a one-way street of people killing whales. The possibility of interspecies communication was raised, people tried to understand how whales think and how they perceive the world, and scientists worked on resolving conflicts between whales and fishermen in coastal waters. People began to actively seek out interactions with whales, who seemed to demonstrate curiosity and humor toward the humans they encountered, and who seemed to have complex social interactions with their own kind.

The question today, as whaling nations are increasingly calling for the resumption of commercial whaling, is whether whaling in any form is acceptable. Should we be killing what we now know to be highly evolved and intelligent creatures when substitutes for almost all whale products exist? As whale scientist Roger Payne observed, "The world has whales that appear to be intelligent, that can sing songs, change those songs, and use rhyme and human laws of composition. They form bubble nets of great intricacy and complexity and cooperatively feed together in clever ways. This is not the sort of animal you should turn into fat and oil and lipstick and margarine and cat food and corset stays."

Today, we are returning to view the whale as an object of awe and majesty, a creature with which we have the privilege to share this earth. Is extermination the most imaginative reaction we can have to a source of such wonder and power? Only time will tell.

Part One

DISCOVERING
WHALES

*Ancient, unknown mammals left the land
In search of food or sanctuary,
And walked into the water.*

*Their arms and hands changed into water-wings;
Their tails turned into boomerang-shaped tail-flukes,
Enabling them to fly, almost weightless, through the oceans;
Their hind-legs disappeared, buried deep within their flanks.*

. . . .

Larger brains evolved, ten times as old as man's.

—Heathcote Williams, *Whale Nation*

Left: *Whales are descended from small, shrewlike
mammals. The whales' ancestors, the primordial
archaeocetes, became amphibious 45 to 50 million years
ago. Thirty-eight to 25 million years ago, two separate
lineages arose: the Odontoceti, toothed whales, and then
the Mysticeti, baleen whales. The closest living relatives of
whales are deer, sheep, and hippopotamuses.
(Photograph © James Gritz)*
Inset: *Renaissance scholar Konrad Gesner carefully
recorded this sixteenth-century view of a whale.*

WHAT IS A WHALE?

Whale classification is an evolving science. Even today it is thought that there are species of beaked whale in the world's oceans that have yet to be identified; scientists have yet to decide whether there are one, two, or three species of right whales; and a new group of killer whales has recently been discovered in the waters off British Columbia that differs from both the resident and transient populations previously identified.

When people first began interacting with whales, they were hazy on the details of whale biology and did not know what kinds of whales they were encountering. Thus, European engravings from the sixteenth century depict strange monsters with spouting funnels, sharp teeth, and snakelike bodies. These early artists had likely never seen a whale and were usually working from the embellished descriptions of frightened sailors.

Whalers in the sixteenth and seventeenth centuries had more reason to identify different species of whales than earlier sailors and explorers, because some whales were more desirable targets than others. The first whale targeted by commercial whalers was the right whale. It swam slowly, yielded a great deal of oil and baleen, and, most importantly, floated when dead. It was the "right" whale to kill. Because they frequent shorelines, humpback whales were another species in widespread contact with early whalers—in nineteenth-century scientific literature there were twenty-three names to describe humpback whales in different parts of the world. When the first sperm whale was killed off the shore of New England in 1712, the whaling captain had no idea what kind of whale he had caught.

Right whales, humpbacks, and sperm whales all belong to the order Cetacea. Cetaceans can be divided into two living suborders: odontocetes or toothed whales and mysticetes or baleen whales. (The third suborder, the archaeocetes, no longer exists.)

Odontocetes (Toothed Whales)

FAMILY	SPECIES
Physeteridae	Sperm Whales
Monodontidae	Narwhals and Belugas
Ziphiidae	Beaked Whales
Delphinidae	Oceanic Dolphins (includes Orcas and Pilot Whales)
Phocoenidae	Porpoises
Platanistidae	River Dolphins

Mysticetes (Baleen Whales)

FAMILY	SPECIES
Balaenidae	Right and Bowhead Whales
Balaenopteridae (rorquals)	Blue, Fin, Sei, Bryde's, Minke, and Humpback Whales
Eschrichtiidae	Gray Whales
Neobalaenidae	Pygmy Right Whale

MYSTERIES OF THE DEEP

As recently as 25 million years ago, the oceans contained toothed whales with serpentine bodies that may have crawled up on land to mate and give birth. It has been suggested that these zeuglodonts could have given rise to the stories of sea monsters and dragons prevalent in legends from around the world.

According to Greek legend, when the Trojan woman Hesione was bound to a rock as a sacrifice to a sea monster, she was rescued by the famed hero Hercules. Hercules's offer to destroy the creature was gratefully accepted by the citizens of Troy, who built a high wall to protect Hercules from the monster as it emerged from the sea and advanced across the plains. When the monster reached the wall, it looked over the top and opened its jaws. Hercules immediately grabbed his weapons and leapt down its throat. He spent three days in the monster's belly before he managed to cut himself out. The struggle to kill the monster is said to have cost him every hair on his head.

In Norse mythology, when Odin, leader of the gods, banished the serpent Jormundgand to the depths of the ocean, the serpent grew so large that he encircled the earth. His thrashings were said to be the cause of storms. Odin's son, Thor, the god of thunder, fought the serpent, who bit him. Before Thor succumbed to Jormundgand's venom, he dealt the serpent a fatal blow, releasing the earth from Jormundgand's evil coil.

In a story from the African country of Mali, a monster from the depths so terrorized a town by a vast lake that the people could fetch water only once a year and then only if they sacrificed a virgin. A foreign prince heard of the beauty of the king's daughter and decided to come and marry her. Unfortunately, that year she was the only virgin left and was to be sacrificed. Undaunted, he traveled to the lake, freed the princess, and slew the monster as it emerged from the depths.

The aquatic monsters of these three stories struck terror in the hearts of all but the bravest souls. Although scientists argue that zeuglodonts died out long ago, the legends persist, as people continue to report sightings of such creatures as the Loch Ness Monster in Scotland and Ogopogo in Canada's Lake Okanagan.

TOOTHED WHALES

Toothed whales tend to be smaller than baleen whales and male odontocetes are sometimes considerably larger than females. (In baleen whales, it is the female who is usually slightly larger than the male.) Toothed whales use echolocation (similar to our ASDIC and SONAR systems) to locate prey. They eat squid, fish, and, in the case of some killer whales, other sea mammals. They appear to form more stable social groups than baleen whales (at least they tend to gather in larger numbers that we can visually identify as groups or pods), and they strand more often than baleen whales. The largest toothed whale is the sperm whale, which is also believed to be the oldest species of whale living today.

Sperm Whales

Sperm whales frequent deep water and eat fish, bottom-feeding sharks, and cephalopods, including enormous squid. A giant squid found intact in the stomach of a 47-foot-long (14.3-m) sperm whale captured near the Azores, in the middle of the North Atlantic Ocean, was 34 feet (10.4 m) long and weighed 400 pounds (182 kg).

The deepest divers of any mammals, sperm whales may descend as

At the depths to which adult sperm whales dive, the pressure may exceed one ton per square inch (0.91 tonnes per 2.5 sq. cm). They can survive this extreme pressure because they are mostly made up of water, which is incompressible, and because they collapse body cavities, such as their lungs, as they dive. (Photograph © Francois Gohier)

deep as two miles (3.2 km) in search of food, and their dives may last for more than two hours. They can dive so deep because their lungs exchange about 90 percent of their contents with each breath (by comparison, human lungs exchange 15 to 20 percent). Also, they have more blood for their body size than humans do, therefore they can store proportionately more oxygen. They can also store more oxygen in their muscle tissue than humans by using a muscle hemoglobin called myoglobin. These high levels of myoglobin give sperm whale meat its characteristic dark color and unpleasant taste.

Living far from shore, sperm whales started to have more than passing encounters with people after they were discovered out on the open seas by eighteenth-century Yankee whalers. This contact continued with modern pelagic whalers until the global moratorium on whaling in 1986. Sperm whales were highly valued by whalers for the liquid wax, or spermaceti oil, that exists in their huge heads. The whales may use this oil for buoyancy while diving and to focus sonar clicks to stun prey.

In the days of old-style whaling, sperm whales gained a reputation for being ferocious and going out of their way to attack boats. Recent research, however, suggests that sperm whales are timid creatures that prefer to give danger a wide berth. The males are often solitary and join the females only for mating before moving on. Females and calves live together in close-knit social groups in deep tropical waters, and mothers stagger their dives so that there is always an adult near the surface to look after the young. If threatened by killer whales, sperm whales put their heads together in a defensive circular formation, known as a marguerite, with the calves in the center.

In his Historia Animalium, *Book IV (1604), Konrad Gesner depicted this hapless sailing vessel harassed by a malevolent-looking creature. With a sea full of such monsters, it's a wonder sixteenth-century sailors ever set foot in a boat.*

Toothed whales, such as sperm whales, are prone to mass strandings, though it is not understood why these whales beach themselves in such large numbers. There are a number of different theories. One suggests that mass strandings often occur at places where the earth's geomagnetic field is anomalous, hampering the whales' ability to navigate. Although no direct evidence exists for biomagnetic navigation in cetaceans, several species are known to possess biomagnetite, the biomineral required to detect magnetic fields, in their brains. Alternatively, on gently sloping beaches the animals' sonar may misjudge the distance to the shoreline. Or they may simply be following prey, or a member of their group that is dying, ashore.

In the 1995 book *Whales, Dolphins and Porpoises*, sperm whale researcher Hal Whitehead observes, "Sperm whales live most of their lives deep in the seas, foraging in a habitat of great pressure and almost total darkness, an environment we understand less well than we understand the surface of the moon." Scientists are attempting to penetrate these depths of ignorance. Today, among other things, they are researching the clicks sperm whales use to communicate with one another (it has also been suggested that sonar clicks stun prey and may cause it to emit bioluminescence, so sperm whales can see and catch it). They are also studying the physiological adaptations that allow these whales to dive to and swim in great depths for extended periods of time.

In his 1969 fictionalized account, *The Year of the Whale*, whale biologist Victor B. Scheffer imagined what it must be like to be a sperm whale descending far beneath the surface in search of food:

> Down, down, on a long, slanting course through the zones of green and purple twilight to utter blackness below. Luminescent fishes and strange blobby creatures brush past his undulating tail as he goes steadily deeper. The pressure is now one hundred tons to the square foot; the water is deathly cold and quiet. At a depth of three thousand feet he levels off and begins to search for prey. The sonar device in his great dome is operating at full peak. Within a quarter-hour he reads an attractive series of echoes and he turns quickly to the left, then to the right. Suddenly he smashes into a vague, rubbery, pulsating wall. The acoustic signal indicates the center of the Thing. He swings open his gatelike jaw with its sixty teeth, seizes the prey, clamps it securely in his mouth, and shoots for the surface. He has found a half-grown giant squid, thirty feet long, three hundred pounds in weight. The squid writhes in torment and tries to tear at its captor, but its sucking tentacles slide from the smooth, rushing body. When its parrot beak touches the head of the whale it snaps shut and cuts a small clean chunk of black skin and white fibrous tissue. The whales shakes its prey in irritation.
>
> Suddenly the surrounding water fills with light and the bull lies puffing in the sunshine. He crushes the squid's central spark of life, its gray tentacles twist and roll obscenely like dismembered snakes.

Orcas

Killer whales or orcas are actually the largest members of the dolphin family. Found in every ocean in the world from pole to pole, they are the most widely distributed mammals on earth. Capable of reaching speeds of 40 mph (64 kph), killer whales are the fastest animals in the sea. Killer whales are highly social and live all their lives in tightly knit matriarchal pods. They are also highly vocal. Members of a pod communicate using a suite of sounds, some of which are shared with other pods and some of which are unique to that pod. There is a correlation between how closely related two pods are and the similarity of their vocal repertoires. The uniqueness of the vocalizations of individual pods may make killer whales the only species other than humans to use true dialects.

One of the most distinctive features of the orca or killer whale is its tall dorsal fin. Scientists use the size and shape of the dorsal fin, along with the patterns of a whale's saddle and eye patches, to identify individual animals. (Photograph © Jeff Foott)

The killer whales that live in the Pacific Northwest are divided into three separate communities. The first two, a northern and a southern community of resident whales, feed on salmon and other fish in coastal waters. The third, a transient community, keeps to itself and ranges farther offshore. The transients live in smaller pods, vocalize less frequently, and eat mainly marine mammals such as seals, sea lions, and, occasionally, dolphins and other whales.

Revered by the Indians of the northwest coast of North America and hunted by some tribes for food, killer whales were reviled by whalers, who were disgusted by their predatory habits. (Killer whales often hung around whaleships in packs, eating the tongues out of the whale carcasses that were lashed to the ships' sides.) People have long feared orcas, but research shows that they are intelligent, social creatures who display friendly behavior towards people in aquaria and in the wild.

Today, people are reevaluating their attitudes towards killer whales and resident pods are the mainstay of the growing whale-watching industry off the northwestern coast of North America. Douglas Hand, in his 1994 book *Gone Whaling*, describes a research vessel coming across orcas off the San Juan islands on the coast of Washington state in the early 1990s:

> We waited, bobbing in the water, squinting, and—
> "kwhoof"—two whales surfaced right in front of the boat....
> Just as quickly as they'd surfaced, they were gone. To the
> front, four or five whales could be seen bearing straight for
> the boat. Another unexpectedly surfaced under the bow,
> announcing himself with a huge exhalation—"kwhoof." I
> could feel the mist and smell it, heavy and oily, as cameras
> whirred on motor drive.... Whales were everywhere around
> the boat, some close, some distant and too far for pictures.
> The water was flat and calm and dotted with dorsal fins and
> "kwhoofs."... Suddenly, off to the left about a hundred yards,
> a whale breached, hurling itself completely out of the water
> and reentering with a heavy splash ..., turning and twisting,
> ebony black and a flash of pearl white etched against a hazy
> blue sky.... As I watched the orca, it was impossible to keep
> myself from imagining the pure pleasure of leaping into the
> air and soaring with them.

Beluga Whales

Beluga whales are small, toothed whales that live in Arctic and subarctic regions. Calves are born dark gray, taking on their yellowish white coloration by the time they reach sexual maturity. The name "beluga" is derived from the Russian word *belukha*, which means white. Unlike other cetaceans, which shed skin continuously, belugas undergo a seasonal molt; they are one of the few whales whose entire skin can be used as leather, although the penile skin of other whales can also be used in this manner.

Belugas as art; the beautiful beluga ballet.
(Photograph © Jeff Foott)

Belugas can be found in the Arctic Ocean, the Sea of Okhotsk, the Bering Sea, the Gulf of Alaska, the Beaufort Sea, Baffin Bay, Hudson Bay, and the Gulf of St. Lawrence, and in the estuaries of large rivers such as the Amur River in Russia and the Yukon and St. Lawrence Rivers in Canada. Often found in water that is barely deep enough to cover their bodies, they sometimes get stranded, having to wait until high tide before they are able to swim away. In the Arctic summer, hundreds of belugas gather in warm, shallow waters to give birth and feed. Relatively slow swimmers, they may fall prey to killer whales or polar bears. They are also hunted by the Aboriginal peoples in northern latitudes.

Belugas may use sound to create acoustical maps of their surroundings and to relay messages about ice conditions to other beluga whales. Whale observer Jim Nollman says listening to beluga vocalizations in Lancaster Sound is like listening to "a raucous party . . . through the walls of an apartment building." Like other cetaceans, belugas do not possess vocal chords; they probably produce their sounds by moving air in their nasal sacs. It is thought that the fat-filled lower jaw bone of the beluga conducts sound waves to the whale's middle ear, supplementing the sounds it may hear through it ears.

The belugas of the St. Lawrence River are indicators of the extent to which urban, agricultural, and industrial pollution is jeopardizing ocean life. Close to the top of the food chain, feeding on fish, crustaceans, and cephalopods from the tainted St. Lawrence, belugas living here are full of potent toxins and display many physical abnormalities. They may contain polychlorinated biphenyls (PCBs), dichlorodiphenyltrichloroethane (DDT), and heavy metals such as lead, mercury, and cadmium. The situation is so bad that in Canada beluga carcasses are treated as toxic waste.

Along with killer whales, belugas are the only great whales to be regularly kept in captivity. In a 1994 *National Geographic* article, whale scientist Kenneth S. Norris described an encounter in an aquarium that piqued his interest in finding out more about these whales in the wild:

> Perfectly white with dark lustrous eyes, the 12-foot-long beluga whale glided up and braked to a stop on the other side of a large window at the Vancouver Aquarium in Canada. Then he did a strange thing.
>
> From the blowhole atop his head he slowly blew a big mushroom-shaped globe of air into the water. Backing away from the rising bubble, he extended his mobile, pursed lips and sucked it into his mouth.
>
> Next the whale puffed the air back into the water ahead of him. He eyed his creation, which expanded as it rose. Then he matter-of-factly sucked it in again.
>
> Not finished yet, he backed away a little and blew the air out once more. This time he nodded his head sharply downward, sending an invisible boil of water against the expanding bubble. It instantly became a twisting bracelet, shining and expanding until it began to break into flattened, rising spheres.

Belugas share with dolphins the slightly upturned corner of the mouth, which makes them look like they are smiling. They, along with narwhals, are also able to turn their heads because the vertebrae in their necks are not fused as they are in other whales. (Photograph © James Gritz)

The long horn sported by male narwhals was once thought to come from the legendary unicorn. It was highly prized because it was thought to have magical properties and to act as an antidote to poison. Edward Topsell in his Historie of Foure-Footed Beastes *(1607) wrote: "I my selfe have herd of a man worthy to be beleeved, that having eaten a poisond cherry, and perceiving his belly to swell, he cured himself by the marrow of this horn being drunke in wine in a very short space."*

Then he sucked up the bubbles, pumped his flukes and was off.

I didn't know what to think. In four decades of studying porpoises, dolphins, and whales all over the world, I'd never seen anything quite like it. Many animals engage in play, but this beluga seemed to be showing an interest in something more like art.

Narwhals

Narwhals are the Arctic whales known for their long, spiral tusks which, in the Middle Ages, were purported to be unicorn horns. The tusk—usually found only on males—is actually one of the narwhals' two upper jaw teeth, which has elongated and grown externally. Narwhal tusks usually grow in a counterclockwise direction; they can grow to be 10 feet (3 m) long and weigh up to 12 pounds (5 kg). Because the tusk is hollow for most of its length, it is quite brittle. The area where the tusk grows through the narwhal's upper lip is usually infected with lice; the tip of the tusk is polished and smooth. The male narwhal's tusk is thought to be too brittle to be used in tusk-to-tusk combat and is more likely a secondary sexual characteristic used to advertise the narwhal's fitness as a prospective mate.

Narwhals live mainly in the High Arctic. Pods of ten to one hundred narwhals can be found in the Davis Strait, Baffin Bay, and in the Greenland Sea, feeding on squid, fish, and crustaceans. Mature narwhals are grayish with dark green, brown, or black smudges. They often swim belly up and may lie motionless for several minutes, hence the name, which comes from the Scandinavian word *nār* meaning "corpse."

Nineteenth-century ethnographer Franz Boas recorded this Inuit tale of the origin of the narwhal. A widow lived in a hut with her young son and daughter. Unfortunately, the boy became blind. Now that he could no longer hunt, the woman treated him badly and often deprived him of food. One day a polar bear stuck its nose into the hut, and the woman ordered her son to shoot it, even though he could not see the bear. His sister helped him by steadying his bow, and he succeeded in killing the bear. The woman, however, pretended that he had missed his mark, and she ordered her daughter to come out with her to butcher the bear and not to tell the boy.

A while later a loon flew overhead and saw the boy. He invited the boy to come with him, and he dove into the water with the boy until the boy's eyesight was restored. When the boy came back to his hut, he saw the bearskin stretched out to dry and asked his mother where it had come from. She said that some hunters had given it to her.

The boy was angry that she had lied to him, and he left the hut to live in the village, where he became a great hunter. When he hunted white whales [belugas], he wrapped the harpoon line around his body so that the whales he harpooned did not escape into the sea.

One day he decided to get his revenge on his mother, and he asked her to help him hunt whales. He wrapped the harpoon line around her body and waited for a large whale to swim by. When he harpooned the whale, he took care not to strike a lethal blow, and the whale dragged his mother out to sea with her hair flowing behind her. She cried out in vain. When the whale surfaced, the boy's mother had been transformed into a black narwhal with a long white tusk.

BALEEN WHALES

The other living suborder of whales are the mysticetes or baleen whales. Baleen whales do not have teeth. Instead they have long, keratinous fringes of a tough, hairlike substance that hang down from their upper jaws. The whales use these fringes of baleen (also sometimes called whalebone) to strain tiny organisms out of sea water. Right and bowhead whales, with their long, fine baleen, eat the smallest planktonic vertebrates of any of the baleen whales. Some baleen whales, especially those with shorter, coarser baleen, like humpbacks and grays, also eat small schooling fish. The largest whale of all, however—the enormous blue—subsists almost entirely on a diet of marine crustaceans no more than three inches long.

Among the great baleen whales are animals that undertake annual migrations from rich summer feeding grounds at the poles to warm winter breeding and calving grounds in the mid-latitudes. While in the Arctic or Antarctic, they eat 3 to 4 percent of their body weight daily to build up a thick layer of blubber. They live off that blubber for the rest of the year, as there is little food for them to eat in the warmer waters where they mate and give birth to their young.

The scientific name for baleen whales, Mysticeti, comes from the Greek word mystax, meaning "mustache," referring to the hairy appearance of the whale's baleen plates. Like fingernails in humans, baleen grows throughout a whale's lifetime, with the terminal end continually wearing off. (Photograph © Brandon D. Cole)

The three main families of baleen whales are grays, rights, and rorquals. The gray whale is the only member of its family. The right whale family includes the right and bowhead whales. The rorqual family, which is distinguished by the grooves along their throats, includes the humpback, blue, fin, and sei whales.

Gray Whales

The only whale that may have been exterminated by the actions of people to date is the Atlantic gray whale, which likely disappeared some time in the seventeenth or eighteenth century. Gray whales along the western coast of North America (which belong to the Pacific stock of gray whales) seem to have made the most of their reprieve from whaling. They have not been hunted commercially since the 1970s, and their numbers are now thought to be at pre-whaling levels; the stock in the western north Pacific, however, is in desperate straits, possibly numbering fewer than two hundred animals.

The gray whale, like the killer whale, has undergone a dramatic transformation in the public consciousness. Known as "devilfish" by early whalers because of the tendency of mother whales to attack boats if they felt their young were in danger, today the gray whales of Baja California are known as "friendly whales." They go out of their way to intercept whale-watching boats, offering their backs and fins to be scratched and even allowing ardent fans to put their hands inside their mouths to stroke their baleen. Gray whales are often covered in barnacles and whale lice, and an individual whale may carry up to half a ton of these hangers-on.

Eastern gray whales undertake the longest migration of any mammal in the world, from the waters of Mexico to Alaska—a distance of 13,000 miles (21,000 km). A 30-ton (27.2-tonne) whale may lose up to 8 tons (7.26 tonnes) of blubber on this journey, which is conducted at an average speed of 115 miles (185 km) per day. These grays are the most easily monitored of whale populations as they swim through the narrow Unimak Pass in the Aleutians on their annual migration, where they can be counted by shore-based observers. The blotchy markings on a gray whale's skin are distinctive enough for scientists to be able to identify individual animals.

Unlike other baleen whales, which feed at or near the surface, gray whales are mainly bottom feeders who use their baleen plates to sift through sediment on the ocean floor. They also feed on small fish in mid-water with occasional lunges to the surface. They do not feed in winter, but begin to feed on their northward migration to their summer feeding grounds. The 1995 book *Whales, Dolphins and Porpoises*, by James D. Darling and others, tells of one particular individual who was observed by scientists in 1984:

> Usually gray [whale]s feed at depth, and visibility is extremely poor. On Easter Sunday of 1984 a gray whale was sighted in Grice Bay, Vancouver Island, a lagoon off one of the protected waterways of outer coast. At low tide, extensive mudflats reduced the water to a few channels. Upon investigation we found a small gray whale, which became known as Quarternote because of a marking on its tail shaped like a musical note. It spent its days in clear, shallow water, filtering mouthfuls of bottom sediments, stopping only to rest and occasionally to rub on nearby shoals. The whale allowed us to hang over the bow of the small boat with mask and snorkel and watch its activity, at times only a few feet away.
>
> Quarternote dived forward, turning on its side like a fighter plane. Reaching the bottom at about a 45-degree angle, the whale plunged the tip of its jaw into the mud and lowered the side of its face and mouth flush to the bottom. Most, if not all, forward movement ceased. Then it would start a gulping-sucking action, obviously expanding and contracting its three throat grooves—an undulating, almost machinelike action of the throat. At times we could see sediment flowing from the corners of its mouth. After a few minutes, Quarternote would stop, turn upright, "chew" by moving jaws and baleen up and down, then—while rising to the surface—shoot streams of sediment from the sides of its mouth, presumably swallowing organisms. After a few breaths Quarternote would repeat the process. When the tide was out, we saw the mudflat dotted with whale-mouth-size craters. The whale had been eating ghost shrimp.

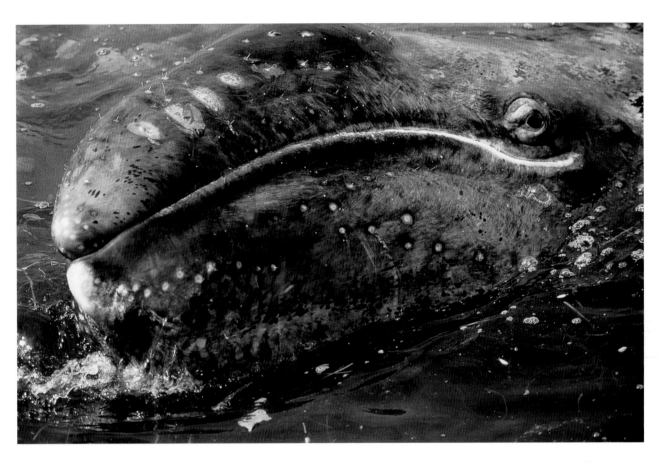

The gray whale is the most primitive of the baleen whales. It has few throat grooves, short baleen plates, and a small dorsal hump followed by a series of bumps rather than a dorsal fin. This friendly gray whale calf was photographed in Magdalena Bay, Mexico. (Photograph © Marilyn Kazmers / SharkSong)

Right Whales

The persecution of the right whale is the closest that humans have come to exterminating a species with a worldwide distribution. From the Basques of the 1100s to the commercial whalers of the eighteenth century, whalers eagerly pursued these fat, slow-moving whales. The hunters must have seen them as traveling containers of blubber and baleen just waiting to be rendered into oil to light the world and incorporated into corsets to satisfy the whims of women's fashion. By about 1900, there were too few right whales left in the oceans of the world for the economic returns from whaling to cover the costs of the hunt, and the species was considered commercially extinct.

The blubber of the right whale is twice as thick as the blubber of most other baleen whales, and right whales weigh more per foot of body length than any other species of whale except the bowhead. The testes of a male right whale have a combined weight of one ton (.91 tonne) and are the largest in the animal world. Right whales also have the broadest tail flukes of any whale, measuring up to 22 feet (7 m) across. According to whale researcher Roger Payne, right whales off the coast of Patagonia use their tails as sails, putting their flukes up in the air and having the wind push them along. The whales then swim back upwind and repeat the exercise, seemingly just for fun.

Right whales were accorded some protection in the early 1930s and theoretically enjoyed full protection by 1937. The northern right whale is likely the most endangered whale in the world today. There may be as few as three hundred left in the North Atlantic and maybe just a few dozen in the North Pacific. DNA studies have shown that the slow birth rate of North Atlantic right whales may be due to inbreeding, partly explaining why the population has yet to recover despite almost a century's reprieve from whaling. A few populations of southern right whales can be found off the southern coasts of Africa and Australia, and along the eastern coast of New Zealand. The largest concentration is a population of southern right whales numbering between three and five thousand off Peninsula Valdes in Argentina.

The Argentine population of southern right whales has been the focus of continuous scientific study since the 1970s. At Peninsula Valdes, a group of right whales comes to breed and give birth their young. They socialize with one another, raise their tails to sail in the wind, and play with seaweed by draping it over their blowholes. On calm winter days the sound of their snores and snuffles fills the air as they doze in the bay. Roger Payne described the antics of some of the whales he was studying:

> Unfortunately the objects right whales play with are not limited to seaweed. We have found this tendency over the years to be an infernal nuisance. For example, when our efforts to erect the single tide gauge thirty-three feet high were foiled by the mother right whale who destroyed it, I decided to build instead a series of stakes along the steeply sloping beach face which we could use to determine the

height of the tide. Of course by now we expected trouble. Sure enough it came. Right whales began to seek out our stakes and break them in such a way that it was obviously intentional. There was one mother who apparently found this kind of activity particularly diverting. She would ease up to one of our tide gauges, moving very, very slowly in the last few meters of her approach, and finally, pressing her head against it, would start beating her tail very slowly up and down, pressing against the stick and causing it to lean more and more until with a snap it gave way. She would then go galumphing off a short way, turn slowly back, search for the next gauge, and break it in exactly the same way. We were not amused.

Bowhead Whales

To the north, in the Arctic, live the bowhead or Greenland whales. The Inuit called them Allaalook, meaning "big stranger." These close relatives of the right whale live out their lives on the edge of the Arctic pack ice. Bowhead whales can break through ice up to 12 inches (30 cm) thick to create breathing holes. Their blubber can reach thicknesses of 28 inches (71 cm) and their baleen, reaching lengths of up to 13 feet (4 m), is the longest of any of the baleen whales. Up to one-third of a bowhead is its enormous head, with a mouth 16.5 to 23 feet (5 to 7 m) long, and lips 5.5 to 6.5 feet (1.7 to 2 m) high. Bowheads can stay underwater for up to forty-five minutes at a time. A 60-ton (54-tonne) bowhead is estimated to eat 1.5 tons (1.4 tonnes) of krill a day. The black dots on the bowhead's chin help scientists identify individual whales.

Once bowheads were the prize of the European Arctic whale fishery. Since 1937 the only hunting of bowheads allowed by the International Whaling Commission has been subsistence hunting by Alaskan Eskimos and the Native people of the Chukchi Peninsula in Siberia. It is estimated that the population of bowheads preceding their exploitation was thirty thousand. Today there may be as few as seven thousand left. Surveys of bowheads in Baffin Bay and Davis Strait suggest that each year only two young are produced for every one hundred whales.

Scientists are recording the sounds that bowheads make and are trying to understand how they communicate as they maneuver through the ice. Christopher W. Clark of Cornell University tracked the movement of bowheads through spring ice off northern Alaska using hydrophones. He reported, "The whales were approaching this massive ice floe. The whales in the lead, the scouts, increased their call rate as they got closer. When they were about half a mile from the ice, they dramatically increased how often they called, as they began to detour around it." Whales nearly a mile behind the advance guard began to detour around the ice before they reached they spot where the scouts had changed the frequency of their calls, implying that the scouts had re–layed information about ice conditions back to the whales that were following.

Individual right whales are identified by the callosities on their heads, which appear in places where people grow hair: on top, on the chin, above the eyes, and on the upper and lower lips. Millions of tiny whale lice give the callosities a red or yellow color, which make them easy for scientists to spot. (Photograph © Jeff Foott)

The head of the humpback is covered with tubercules, which are knoblike protuberances each containing a single, stiff hair. Some researchers think these hairs may function rather like a cat's whisker. Whalers called these knobs "stovebolts." (Photograph © Francois Gohier)

Humpback Whales

The scientific name for this whale, Megaptera, means "big wing," referring to their enormous fins. Humpback pectoral fins can be one-third as long as their bodies, making humpbacks highly maneuverable. They are the only great whales known to be able to swim backwards, and they breach easily and often. Herman Melville, in *Moby-Dick*, described them as "gamesome and lighthearted."

Humpback whales were shunned at first by whalers because they were not as fat as right whales and their baleen was not as long; however, as right whales declined in number, shore fisheries began to decimate humpback populations around the world. Shore whaling was an efficient way to catch these whales, as their migrations are the most predictable of all whales and often bring them close to land. The depredations on their populations after World War II were particularly severe, although humpback whales in the Southern Hemisphere were afforded protection from pelagic whalers in 1938.

Today humpback whales are the focus of a growing whale-watching industry. They are friendly and acrobatic, and their shore-loving habits make them favorites with people who wish to experience the majesty of whales firsthand. It is these same shore-loving habits that cause problems with commercial fishermen, however. Researchers in Newfoundland, for example, spend many hours disentangling humpback whales from the nets of cod fishermen. Scientists are currently devising acoustical devices to warn the whales away from these expensive pieces of equipment.

In the late 1960s, it was discovered that male humpback whales sing long, hauntingly beautiful songs. They appear to use rhymelike repetition to remember their songs, and their "compositions" follow patterns similar to those used by human musicians. Males in a particular breeding area sing the same song, which changes continuously over time. Their songs may proclaim their breeding fitness to potential partners and rivals. When humpbacks sing, they take a stationary position in the water with their heads pointed downward. An individual song may last for up to half an hour and a whale may sing it continuously for hours or even days at a stretch. Several minutes of recorded humpback songs were included on the two Voyageur spacecraft launched in 1977 to tour the solar system before setting forth into the unknown.

Humpback whales often cooperate with one another to catch schools of fish. By releasing bubbles underwater, they create bubble clouds or bubble nets to confuse or trap their prey, using different sized bubbles for different sized prey. They then lunge through the concentrations of fish, taking mouthfuls of fish and water and straining the water out through their baleen. Some individuals slap their tails on the water as they begin to feed, perhaps to create more bubbles or to stun the fish.

This ringside account of humpbacks feeding was published by Cynthia D'Vincent in 1989:

> When a small boat is sitting dead in the water, problems
> may arise. Whales are very much aware of what is going on
> around them, but they rely to a great extent upon their

Humpbacks are rorquals, from the Norwegian word meaning "furrow." The furrows or grooves in a rorqual's throat allow it to take large quantities of sea water into its mouth. The whale then uses its tongue to push the water out through its baleen, which acts like a huge sieve, trapping marine organisms or small fish inside the whale's mouth. This group of about twenty humpbacks has gathered to feed cooperatively on herring. (Photograph © Brandon D. Cole)

hearing, and once they begin feeding they tend to ignore anything other than the capture of their prey. Many a time when sitting quiet in the water I have accidentally taken a solitary feeding whale by surprise. On the other hand, there have also been times when a cooperative feeding group has taken me by surprise.

On one such occasion, I was sitting in our 13-foot Boston Whaler observing a group of nine whales as they worked together over the reef. My boat was dead in the water with a hydrophone over the side. It was a quiet day with not a breath of wind to disturb the glassy water or the heavy air. Whales were swimming along the surface, leisurely blowing their peaceful blows as they foraged for prey. Locating a dense school, they would exhale more forcefully and one by one fluke up and disappear. Sometimes as many as five minutes passed before the eerie vocalizations began. While the whales were singing, I scanned the placid water for any sign of where they might surface. Sometimes they blew a bubble net simultaneously with the song, and then I knew for sure where they would come up. More often there was no sign at all, except in that fraction of a second before they emerged, when thousands of herring flew into the air in a last attempt to escape. The whales would then burst through the surface in a powerful lunge with mouths wide open. Those herring that escaped the jaws of one whale fell victim to the next, as the water from the immense jaws rushed from whale to whale. Their huge ventral pleats were expanded with the intake, then the expelled water gushed out through the baleen plates. The turbulence diminished as the whales resumed their search, and once again fluked up for another encircling of their prey. Over and over again the performance was repeated as they tirelessly worked the productive reef. Each time I guessed fairly accurately when they would surface, always trying to keep a safe distance.

The day had been long. I was parched and burnt after many hours out in the small boat, and decided to head back to the ship. The whales had been down for a long time, and then I began to hear the song without the aid of the hydrophone. At once all of the nearby herring stopped their surface swimming. An ominous silence fell upon the stillness of the day. I had been expecting the whales to surface at least a quarter of a mile away, but the fact that I could hear their song unaided meant that they were near. Nervously I glanced over the side of the boat just in time to see the white flash of pectoral fins racing to the surface. If I wasn't engulfed, I would be crushed. Nine whales together add up to some 700,000 pounds. My little boat weighed 400. The odds did not look good. I grabbed my camera as the whales broke through and snapped a picture—as I thought, my last.

Tremendous jaws encased my boat, baleen surrounded me
and herring shot through the air, landing at my feet. Within a
split second, the whales saw me and they veered, collided,
then sank back into the deep. I was left intact, swamped and
shaken, amid excited blows all around.

Blue, Fin, and Sei Whales

Until the late nineteenth century, the largest of the swift-swimming
rorquals—the blue, fin, and sei whales—lived out their lives in relative
peace. Sailing boats could not keep up with them and if by chance one
was struck by a harpoon, it would sink out of the whalers' grasp. In the
early part of this century all this changed. Steam ships could chase down
these magnificent creatures, exploding harpoons could kill them efficiently, and techniques were invented to inflate the carcasses with air so
they would not sink. Once caught, they were hauled up the stern
slipways of huge, pelagic factory ships.

Blues, fins, and seis are basically three size variations of the same body
pattern. Sei whales are the smallest of the three and do not swim as far
north or as far south as the other two. Sei whales have enormous eye-
balls—12 inches (30.5 cm) in circumference. The most versatile feeders
of all rorquals, they feed on krill, copepods, and some squid. They usually
gulp their food, but they are also the only rorqual to skim feed like right
whales. Whalers turned their attentions to sei whales in the late 1950s
after stocks of fins and blues had been severely depleted.

Fin whales are known as the greyhounds of the ocean, attaining
speeds of up to 37.5 miles per hour (46 kph) when accelerating through
schools of fish. They are the only mammals with consistently asymmetri-
cal markings, white on one side of the jaw and black on the other.
Individuals are identified by the pigmentation on their head and back
behind their blowholes. Fin whales feed on krill and small schooling
fish. In 1969, the International Whaling Commission introduced species
quotas for catches of fin and sei whales—the first species quotas in
the world.

The largest of all the whales is the blue whale. From the moment of
their conception until they are weaned at the age of seven months, baby
blue whales are the fastest-growing organisms on earth. The 2-ton (1.8-
tonne) blue whale fetus develops in less than eleven months—the time it
takes to grow a 12-pound (5.4-kg) baby porpoise. Once it is born, every
day for the next seven months, the baby blue whale consumes more than
100 gallons (379 l) of fat-rich milk, puts on 250 lbs (114 kg)—more
than 10 lbs (4.5 kg) an hour—and grows an inch or more (2 to 3 cm).
The growth rate of a baby blue whale is almost visible to the naked eye
and is twenty times the rate at which a human baby grows.

An adult blue whale may eat as much as 8 tons (7.3 tonnes) of krill a
day during the Antarctic summer, putting on weight at a rate of 1 ton
(.91 tonne) every ten days. It is estimated that it takes 2,200 pounds
(1,000 kg) of food to fill an adult blue whale's stomach.

In 1946, whaling countries around the world were allotted whaling
quotas in the form of Blue Whale Units (BWUs) and what better way to

A blue whale slips beneath the water. A 90-foot (27.4-m) blue whale suspended in the ocean experiences enormous differences in pressure from its tail to its head. The whale accommodates the pressure differentials thanks to a complex system of valves known as the retia mirabile *(wonderful nets) and a 2-ton (1.8-tonne) heart that beats slowly, pumping approximately 60 gallons (227 l) of blood with every beat. (Photograph © Marilyn Kazmers/SharkSong)*

The calls of the blue and fin whales are the loudest attributed to any animal. Using no more energy than radiates from a thirty-watt light bulb, blue whales may emit sounds capable of traveling thousands of miles through deep sound channels in the ocean. We do not know to what extent sound pollution from shipping and other human activities may interfere with these solitary whales' ability to find each other over long distances and to breed. (Photograph © Mike Johnson/Innerspace Visions)

fill this unit than by catching blue whales—much less work than filling the quota with larger numbers of smaller species. The blue whales did not stand a chance. Today, some populations of the largest animal ever to have lived may have passed the point of no return and may never recover.

Blue whales communicate with sonic booms that may travel several thousand miles through deep sound channels in the ocean. These sounds may be for communication; they may also help blue whales create a sound map of the ocean. With the help of hydrophones originally installed by the United States Navy to track Soviet submarines, marine scientists today are researching the low-frequency sounds made by blue whales and trying to ascertain the extent to which sound pollution in the ocean may interfere with blue whales' ability to find one another to breed.

This extract from the journal of Doctor J. D. B. Stillman of San Francisco relates an encounter with a blue whale in the days before these enormous animals were routinely hunted by whalers. The *Plymouth* was on a voyage from San Francisco to Central America in 1850, and for twenty-four consecutive days the huge whale stayed close by the ship:

> November 13th: We are witnesses of a very remarkable exhibition of the social disposition of the whale. A week ago today, we passed several, and during the afternoon it was discovered that one of them continued to follow us, and was becoming more familiar, keeping under the ship and only coming out to breathe. A great deal of uneasiness was felt, lest in his careless gambols he might unship our rudder, or do us some other damage. It was said that bilge-water would drive him off, and the pumps were started, but to no purpose. At length more violent means were resorted to; volley after volley of rifle-shots were fired into him, billets of wood, bottles, etc., were thrown upon his head with such force as to separate the integument; to all of which he paid not the slightest attention, and he still continued to swim under us, keeping our exact rate of speed, whether in calm or storm, and rising to blow almost into the cabin windows. He seems determined to stay with us until he can find better company. . . .
>
> November 29th: . . . We long since ceased our efforts to annoy him, and had become attached to him as to a dog. We had named him "Blowhard," and even fancied, as we called him, that he came closer under our quarter, when I felt like patting his glabrous sides, and saying: "Good old fellow." As the water grew shoaler he left us, with regret unfeigned on our part, and apparently so on his.

Kolevig

Bredevig

Rauga Iand

Huala tuo

Barrd

Baraaftrang

Vadil

Vartr̄Sakr.

Kerlin

Kallafiord

Foitafiord

Krosfiord

Gilsfiord

Huams

Pelle strand

Flatey

Binꞔeyar

Breydafiordur

Occidens.

C.

Huams fiord

Altafiord

Skegur ftrand.

Hrumfiord

Kolgurfiord

Grinsfia fiord

Galmla vig

Helga peft.

Meyra fnei.

Thallarfiord

Kumbrum vig

Brimnes

Sneuels Iokul.

D.

Ondvertnes

Stapi

Stadarfted

Hersey

Londranga

Haffiorderey

Rosn

G.

E.

Ryk

Eldey

F.

Geie fuelasker

Geie eiar

5   10   15   20

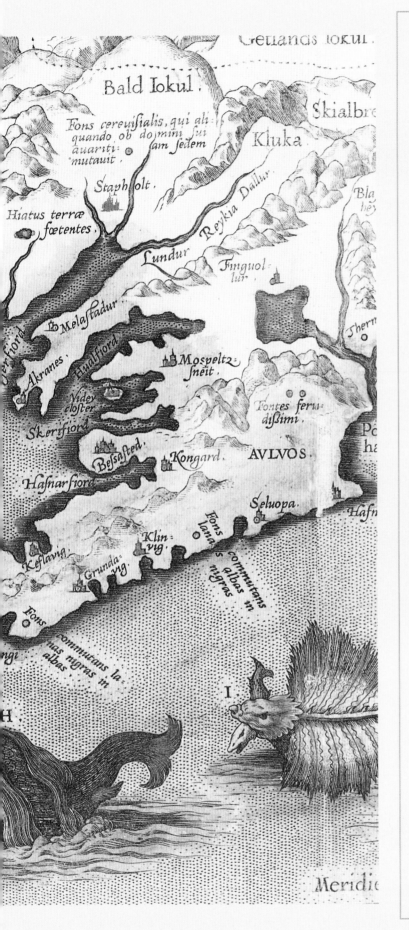

Part Two

OF WHALES AND GODS

Out of night, born the sea,
Out of night, born the God.
Nurtured by the oceans,
Deep and vast his domain.
Into his true nature he formed himself . . .
Life enduring in the sea.
O, Kanaloa
O, ivory-toothed whale.

**—Adapted by Kawena Johnson from the *Kumulipo*,
a Hawaiian creation chant**

Left: *This map by Abraham Ortellius (1527–1598)
depicts the sixteenth-century European view of whales.
Different coastal cultures from around the world wove their
own stories around these awesome creatures whose presence
or absence might mean the difference between life and
death, or who were just too huge to be ignored. (Courtesy
of The Mariners' Museum, Newport News, Virginia)*
Inset: *Stylized orca designs from the Tlingit, Kwakiutl,
and Haida cultures. The exaggerated dorsal fin is typical of
killer whale designs from peoples of the Pacific Northwest.*

ORIGINS AND CONNECTIONS

The Netselik Eskimo tell of Sedna, the enormous daughter of the creator-god Aguta. Aguta was angry with his huge daughter because she had refused to marry the man he had chosen for her. The two were in a boat together, and Aguta decided to get his revenge by throwing his daughter overboard. When she tried to climb back into the boat, he cut off the tops of her fingers, which fell into the sea and became seals. Still she clung to the side of the boat. To make her let go, Aguta cut off the rest of her fingers, which fell into the sea and became walruses. Still Sedna held on. Desperate, Aguta cut off her hands. Unable to hold onto the boat any longer, Sedna abandoned herself to the depths. Her severed hands fell into the water after her and became whales. The explorer K. Rasmussen records that Sedna "became the most feared of all spirits, the most powerful and the one who more than any other controls the destiny of men. . . . Almost all taboo is directed against her, though only in the dark period when the sun is low, and it is cold and windy on earth, for then life is most dangerous to live."

For the tribes of the North American Pacific Northwest, people had the power to call whales into being. In a Tsimshian story recorded by ethnographer Franz Boas, a man called Potlach-Giver got his wife to fetch his adze and his hammer from his village. With his adze, he chopped down a cedar tree and carved from it two killer whales. He rubbed charcoal made from red cedar on their backs; he rubbed lime on their bellies. He took them down to the lake, where they began to swim and dive, but then they both died. Potlach-Giver tried again. This time he chopped down a big yellow cedar. Again he carved two killer whales, while his wife burned food, fat, tobacco, the down of birds, and red ochre as offerings to her husband's success. When Potlach-Giver took these two killer whales down to the lake, they did not die. He then whistled to them and took them down to the ocean, where they swam away.

For the Maori of New Zealand, whales originated in the sky. The Maori sea-god, Tangaroa, had a son, Punga, who was the father of the whales. When a man called Tawhaki climbed to the skies to avenge the murder of his father by Punga's family, he found the whales and threw them down into the sea.

The Aborigines of Australia believed whales had a celestial connection as well. In their mythology, the Rainbow Serpent was a life force associated with the elements—earth, air, fire, and water. The Rainbow Serpent was thought to originate in the Milky Way, and coastal peoples in Australia often symbolized this life force as a whale. Many coastal rock formations were described as the work of the sacred whale, whose energy Aborigines sought to harness through song.

For many cultures familiar with whales, the boundaries between whales and land and whales and people were easily transcended. Storytellers Asatchaq and Samaruna, Inuit who lived on the Tikigaq peninsula in Alaska, described to author and researcher Tom Lowenstein how Tulunigraq, the Raven shaman, caught a whale who became part of their land:

A wooden ladle from the Tsimshian culture of coastal British Columbia. The ladle is carved in the shape of a whale with a humanlike face on the front of the tail. Many cultures felt a strong affinity for the animals with whom they shared their world. (Courtesy of the Canadian Museum of Civilisation, photo numbers S72-1574 and S72-1575)

For the Haida of the Pacific Northwest coast of North America, the killer whale is a bridge to the world of myth. (Photograph ©
Francois Gohier)

Asatchaq:
[Tulunigraq] travelled by kayak.
Then he stopped.
Tulunigraq heard something.
An animal was breathing.
It had risen.
It was breathing.
Raven went closer.
There was something on the surface.
It stretched to the horizon.
Tulunigraq waited.
When its head rose to breathe,

Samaruna:
Nauligaa!: he struck it!
He harpooned the animal.
It dived with Raven's drag-float.
When he saw the animal had dived,
he sang to make it rise.

Uivvaluk! Uivvaluk! Uivvaluk!
Round! Round! Round!

Asatchaq:
The whale-float went round.
And the mask on the float
sang back to Raven.

Samaruna:
The animal surfaced.
The whale came up dry.
It rose in the water.

Asatchaq:
Dry land! *Nuna!*
It was dry land.
It was Tikigaq.
✧ ✧ ✧
Samaruna:

. . . .

When Tulunigraq struck,
the whale became land.
You can still see the wound-hole.

It's a hollow in the tundra
where the grass grows long.

In the summer I will show you.

Whale charms from Alaska carved from (top to bottom) bone, stone, ivory, and wood. For cultures that depended on whales for food, hunting these enormous creatures was a complicated and dangerous procedure that involved much ritual preparation. (Courtesy of the Canadian Museum of Civilisation, photo numbers S75-5870, S75-5871, S75-5872, S75-5873)

43

For the tribes of the Pacific Northwest, whales might shift shape and become people or people might become whales. This traditional tale was recounted to writer Pamela Whitaker in the late 1970s by James Wallas, hereditary chief of the Quatsino Band of the Kwakiutl of northern Vancouver Island:

A man had four daughters. The eldest was eighteen. Every day the girls walked on the beach to a sandy point where they liked to sit and look at the sea.

One day some killer whales went by while the girls were sitting on the point. The eldest girl said, "I'm going to talk to those whales."

"No, you had better not," advised a younger sister.

But the girl did not listen to her sister. She called to the whales, "Killer Whale, come on in. We want a ride." The next thing they knew, a killer whale was right up on the beach.

"Do you think you know how to use this canoe?" he asked.

"I'd sure like to try," answered the eighteen-year-old girl.

"Come on in then," said the whale and opened his big mouth. The girl went through his mouth and into his body. He showed her the interior of his tail and fins and how to use them. He took her for a ride in the water.

"This is fun," cried the girl as they skimmed across the waves and down through the deep water.

When they came back to shore the whale said, "How about your sisters? Would they like a ride?"

"It's lots of fun," the oldest girl called to her sisters. "Why don't you try it?"

The second sister was not interested. The third sister would not try it either, but the youngest said, "I'm going to give it a try."

She went through the whale's mouth and into his interior but could not move his parts properly. Killer Whaler said to her, "Go and tell your older sister to come and try it again."

So the eldest girl went inside the killer whale. They swam away and did not return. The three younger girls waited a long time, then went home and told their mother what had happened. "How are we going to get her back?" the mother wondered.

When the father heard what had happened, he took his canoe and searched out on the water. He looked for many days for his daughter but could not find her.

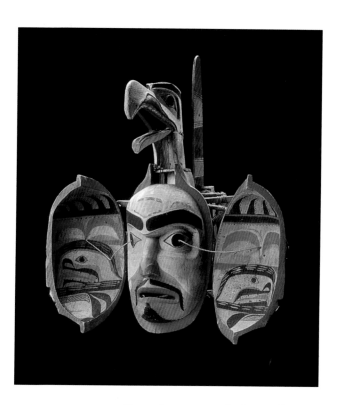

Opposite page and above: *For many cultures of the Pacific Northwest, whales shift shape into people and people shift shape into whales. This Haida transformation mask from 1879 depicts a whale and a seagull. When the mask is opened, a humanlike face is revealed. (Courtesy of the Canadian Museum of Civilisation, photo numbers S92-4172 and S92-4174)*

One day after he had given up the search, one of his younger daughters was walking on the beach. Her lost sister swam up to her and said, "Go and tell my parents I am married now to the killer whale." She was never seen again.

Many coastal cultures attributed their origins to whales. A ghost orca brought culture to the Haida of Canada's Queen Charlotte Islands. The Maori tell of their ancestors traveling from their mythical homeland, Hawaiki, to New Zealand on the backs of whales. The Australian giant Numa Numa appeared to the Gunwingga in Arnhem Land in the form of a whale and taught them how to paint and dance. The Kondoledjeri in southern Australia believed that they were descended from whales. Rainbows in the ocean spray rising from blowholes in the cliffs confirmed their connection with an ocean past. They called to their guardians from these cliffs and when the whales appeared, they danced and sang for them in celebration of their ancestral ties.

Whales' ties extended to other animals as well. The Mirning relate that the animals who came to live in Australia traveled to their new home in the only craft large enough to hold them—Whale's canoe. When migratory birds told the animals of a beautiful empty land across the sea, the animals decided they wanted to visit this land and asked Whale if they could use his canoe. Whale, however, refused. The animals then asked Starfish if he would distract Whale while they borrowed the canoe. Starfish agreed and lulled Whale into a deep sleep by gently picking the whale lice off his skin.

When Whale woke up and realized that his canoe was gone with all the animals in it, he was furious. He flicked Starfish away with one swipe of his mighty tail, but not before Starfish had gouged a hole in Whale's back, a mark which all of Whale's ancestors carry to this day. To escape the wrath of Whale, Starfish and his descendants retreated to the small pools and dark caves of the ocean. Meanwhile Whale set off in pursuit of the animals. Koala with his strong arms was able to paddle the canoe fast enough to keep just ahead of the angry Whale. As soon as the animals reached Australia, they jumped out of the canoe, broke its frame, and threw the wrecked craft into the sea, where it turned into a rocky island. Whale swam up and down the shore, and every year his descendants do so still.

The Haida of the Pacific Northwest believed that killer whales had the power to give them strength, good health, and wealth; women brought their children down to the shore to bathe their feet in the surf from passing pods of killer whales. The Kwakiutl in the same region of the world prayed to killer whales to give them food and placed offerings of mountain goat tallow, cedar bark, or tobacco in the sea. A dead killer whale that washed up on shore was treated with great reverence. In his book, *The Religion of the Kwakiutl Indians,* published in 1930, Franz Boas recorded this "Prayer of a Man Who Finds a Dead Killer Whaler":

Oh, it is great how you lie there on the ground,

Great Supernatural One.
What has made you unlucky?
Why, great and good one, are you lying here
    on the ground?
Friend, Supernatural One,
Why have you been unlucky, friend, for I
    thought you
could never be overcome, by all the
    Short-Life-Maker Women.
Now, you great and good one, have you been overcome
by the one who does as he pleases to us, friend.
I mean this, that you may wish that I shall
    inherit
your quality of obtaining easily all kinds
    of game
and all kinds of fish,
you Great Supernatural One, friend,
you Long-Life Maker.
And also that you protect me,
that I may not have any trouble, Supernatural
    One,
And also that it may not penetrate me,
the evil word of those who hate me among my
    fellow men,
And that only may penetrate themselves
the curses of those who wish me to die quickly.
I mean this, friend,

These Nuu-chah-nulth baskets with whale motifs were woven by folk artist Cecilia Williams using swamp grass and cedar bark. (Courtesy of the Canadian Museum of Civilisation, photo number S84-4217)

Scenes from a Clayoquot whale hunt in the North American Pacific Northwest, drawn by F. N. Wilson for Indian Days of the Long Ago *by historian Edward S. Curtis (1915).*

Only have mercy on me
that nothing evil may befall me,
Great Supernatural One, says he.
"Wâ, I will do this," says the man
on behalf of the one he found dead.

BOUNTY OF THE GODS

Coastal peoples around the world who depended on the carcasses of stranded whales for food were careful to show their appreciation to their gods for this bounty and to share their good fortune throughout the community. In the Annam region of Vietnam, the man to sight a stranded whale honored the animal by dressing in a straw hat and a white robe with the long sleeves turned inside out to signify mourning. The people of the community burned perfume, kindled incense, set off firecrackers, and scattered leaves of gold and silver on the ground in the whale's honor before butchering the carcass and burying the bones in the sand. A small shack was built near the site of the stranding where offerings could be made.

For the Maoris of the South Island of New Zealand, Irakau was a woman who had great power over the creatures of the ocean, including the whales. Irakau was an ancestor of the Waitaha people. At Rangiriri, where the Waitaha lived, a large sand dune covered with grass was thought to be a physical representation of the life force of whales. The Waitaha believed that if someone died and the correct rituals were observed, a whale would swim towards the sand dune and offer itself to the people. The tohunga, or high priest, would then swallow a mouthful of sea water, the whale's element, so that the whale would be unable to return to the sea and the people could feast on its flesh. If the people behaved themselves and shared the feast equitably, all was well. If they quarreled, the tohunga sent the whale back into the sea. If they quarreled while the whale was being cooked, the meat became inedible.

For the Maori, as for the Haida, whales signified wealth and abundance. High-ranking men were likened to sperm whales. The Maori had frequent disputes over coastal areas where whales commonly stranded. Individuals who did not treat these potent symbols with respect deserved to be punished. The story of Kae tells of one such man.

Kae came to the home of his friend Tini-rau to perform ceremonies for one of Tini-rau's children. When Kae wished to return home, Tini-rau lent him his pet whale. He gave Kae instructions about how to treat the whale, but Kae disregarded them, running the whale up onto the beach. Kae then killed the whale, cut it up, and cooked the flesh to share with his friends. Tini-rau waited in vain for many days for the whale to return. Then when the smells of roasted whale flesh were brought to him on the south wind, Tini-rau sent women to find Kae, telling them they would recognize Kae by his broken tooth. The women went to where Kae was and danced and sang comic songs to make all the men open their mouths in laughter. Once they spotted Kae's broken tooth, they recited a charm to send the company to sleep. Then they kidnapped the sleeping Kae and brought him back to Tini-rau's home, where they

HOW OMAL AND THE WHALE
VANQUISHED THE THUNDERBIRDS

Many tales from the Pacific Northwest relate that the Thunderbird could snatch whales right out of the water; a bird so big and strong could surely grasp people right out of their canoes. In this Kwakiutl tale, recorded by Franz Boas in 1910, a man named Omal decides to free his people from the threat of the Thunderbirds by disguising himself as a whale. To carry out his plan, he enlists the help of Mink, Whale, Wasp, Grizzly Bear, Wolf, Black Bear, and Squid. First Omal built a whale out of poles. Then he sent Mink to borrow Whale's mask to give life to the pole whale he had made. Whale gave Mink his mask in a bag, and Mink took the mask to Omal and the other animals. When they all climbed into the pole whale, Mink said he would be in the spout hole. The pole whale went down and came up below the Thunderbirds' house. The father of Thunderbird was sitting on the ground when he saw Omal's whale. He put on his Thunderbird mask and flew out over the ocean to grasp the pole whale. Mink found himself in the

grip of the Thunderbird's talons. As Thunderbird tried to lift the whale out of the water, Wasp stung him in the eye and then Grizzly Bear and Wolf killed him. Then Two-whale Carrier put on his Thunderbird mask and tried to pull the whale out of the water. He too was killed. Three-whale Carrier did not fare much better. He lifted the whale higher out of the water, but he was killed by Grizzly Bear, Wolf, and Black Bear. His face was covered by Squid. Four-whale Carrier succeeded in carrying the pole whale to the beach by the Thunderbirds' house, but then he fell and the animals killed him as well. Omal and his people could now go canoeing without fear of being carried away by Thunderbird.

Reproductions of Thunderbird and Whale designs from the Nuu-chah-nulth or Nootka (top) and Kwakiutl (bottom) cultures. Both designs depict a Thunderbird carrying off a whale. The Nuu-chah-nulth design dates from 1850. It was painted on cedar planks displayed at potlatches. The original for the Kwakiutl design was found in about 1873, painted on the façade of a house in Alert Bay, off the northeastern shore of Vancouver Island.

constructed a replica of the hut in which they had charmed him. In the hut, they built a bed of leaves and ferns over heated rocks. When Kae woke up, he was still a little dazed. The women enticed him over to the bed of ferns, and when he sat down, the women poured water over the leaves. The hot rocks turned the water to steam and Kae was scalded to death.

THE RITUALS OF THE WHALE HUNT

Although some coastal peoples feasted on whale meat only when whales stranded or when dead whales washed up on shore, others hunted whales on a regular basis to provide their communities with the necessities of life. The hunt for the whale required a great deal of courage, and the rituals before and after the hunt were as important as the hunt itself. Despite their extensive preparations, hunters often came home empty handed.

The Nuu-chah-nulth or Nootka, whose traditional territories are on western Vancouver Island in British Columbia, Canada, believed that the great Thunderbird carried Lightning Snakes under his wings. When a whale surfaced, he threw down these Lightning Snakes to kill it. He then plucked the whale out of the sea with his talons and flew away.

A Kwakiutl whale mask of wood, hide, and rope collected by ethnographer George Hunt in 1901. (Neg. no. 4587, courtesy of the Department of Library Services, American Museum of Natural History)

The Nuu-chah-nulth painted Lightning Snakes on the prows of their sea-going canoes and then painted them over with black paint so that the whales would not see them. They believed that by doing this they were harnessing the whale-hunting prowess of the Thunderbird for themselves.

For the Nuu-chah-nulth, the whale hunt embodied many of the checks and balances on which their societies depended for survival. Writing for a 1998 issue of *Ethnology*, Michael Harkin notes that only chiefs could hunt, and their hunts would only be successful if they maintained a moral and ritual purity. The chief who did not exercise self-discipline in preparing for the hunt or who did not support his people with the proceeds of the hunt had to pass his whale magic on to others.

In his 1916 volume *The North American Indian (Nootka)*, ethnologist Edward S. Curtis describes the chief's preparations for the whale hunt. The chief first went to a lake to bathe, rubbing his skin with hemlock twigs. He repeated this ritual daily until the four bunches of twigs he had taken with him were worn out. He then dove deep in the lake and remained underwater as long as he could—sometimes until his eardrums burst. He did this four times. Each time as he came up he blew a mouthful of water to the center of the lake, imitating the sound of a whale. Using slow and deliberate movements, he acted out the way he wished the whale to behave during the hunt. Sometimes his wife would fasten a line around his waist while the chief made the undulating movement of a harpooned whale.

While he underwent this ritual, the chief offered prayers to the whale:

> Whale, I want you to come near me, so that I will get hold of your heart and de– ceive it, so that I will have strong legs and not be trembling and excited when the whale comes and I spear him. Whale, you must not run out to sea when I spear you. Whale, if I spear you, I want my spear to strike your heart. Harpoon, when I use you, I want you to go to the heart of the whale. Whale, when I spear at you and miss you, I want you to take hold of my spear with your hands. Whale, do not break my canoe, for I am going to do good to you. I am going to put eagle-down and cedar bark on your back.

If the hunt was successful, another prayer was recited to the harpooned whale:

> Whale, I have given you what you wish to get—my good harpoon. And now you have it. Please hold it with your strong hands. Do not let go. Whale, turn toward the fine beach of Yahksis, and you will be proud to see the young men come down on the fine sandy beach of my village of Yahksis to see you; and the young men will say to one another: "What a great whale he is! What a fat whale he is! What a strong whale he is!" and you, Whale, will be proud of all that you will hear them say of your greatness. Whale, do not turn outward, but hug the shore, and tow me to the beach of my village of Yahksis, for when you come ashore there, young men will cover your great body with bluebill duck feathers, and with the down of the great eagle, the chief of all birds; for this is what you are wishing, and this is what you are trying to find from one end of the world to the other, every day you are traveling and spouting.

This account of the ritual surrounding the Clayoquot whale hunt in the Pacific Northwest was told to Curtis in 1915:

> When my father was preparing to hunt whales, he lived in the forest for four months, and then sent word to eight men who were his helpers, to go also to the forest and make their

This petroglyph from Olympic National Park in Washington state testifies to the ages-old relationship between the Makah and the sea. In the Makah culture, whale hunting was a privilege reserved for hereditary chiefs and their sons. (Photo-graph © Jeff Foott)

"Whale Hunters Under Sail" by James Kivetoruk Moses (1900–1982), an Eskimo artist from the Seward Peninsula in Alaska. (Courtesy of the Anchorage Museum of History and Art)

bodies pure, that they might have good fortune in capturing a whale. At the appointed time they all came from the woods, got into their great whale canoe, and started far out upon the open water. It was in the springtime, when the whales are not angry. As they started they sang many songs. My father had a hundred whale songs. As they went, my mother and all the women climbed upon the house-tops, singing and beating time on the roof with sticks.

The spear used by my father was not much longer than his body. Its cutting point was a large mussel-shell held in place with the gum of the pine. The rope fastened to the harpoon was of the bark of the cedar. Fastened to this strong rope were many floats made of air-filled skins of the hair-seal. These floated and dragged in the water, and made the whale tired while he swam or tried to dive.

The whaling canoe left the smooth bay and went out into the Great Water. The canoe looked no larger than one's hand.

Sometimes on the hunt they would not find a whale on the first day, but would have to keep paddling about through the night. In the dark they would hear many whales splashing and blowing water into the sky. Then when daylight came they might see one close by.

On sighting a whale they quickly paddled near enough to spear him. If he heard them and sank, they watched closely for him to come to the surface. At last they came near enough to throw harpoons into his body, and as he sank they sang songs to him, praying that he would not be angry. When he came up they harpooned him again, each time fastening more floats to his body.

Perhaps it would take a whole day to kill a single whale, and when he was dead they had hard work to get him home. When at last they towed him to the village, there was great rejoicing; for there would be plenty of food for every one.

The Inuit hunted whales from slender, fragile kayaks or from umiaks capable of transporting many whalers and large amounts of whale meat. In places where sufficient whales were caught, the Inuit could establish permanent winter settlements. This photograph shows a seat from an Inuit whale-hunting boat. (Courtesy of the Anchorage Museum of History and Art)

After killing a whale, the Inuit of Bering Strait would not work for four days while the spirit of the whale was still in its body. No pointed instrument, which might injure the whale's spirit, could be used in the village, nor could the villagers make loud noises that might frighten or offend the whale. Anyone who cut into the dead whale's body with an iron axe would die.

In the Aleutian islands, men hunted whales from kayaks. A ritual preparation of poisonous aconite from the monkshood plant was spread on the head of a dart that was thrown into the whale with the help of a throwing board. The target was a spot just behind the left flipper, to a

THE GIFT OF THE WHALE

When the Great Spirit created this land, he made many beautiful and good things. He made the sun and moon and stars. He made the wide land, white with snow, and the mountains and the ocean. He made fish of all kinds and the many birds. He made the seals and the walrus and the great bears. Then the Great Spirit made the Inupiaq. He had a special love for the people and showed them how to live, using everything around them.

Then, after making all this, the Great Spirit decided to make one thing more. This would be the best creation of all. The Great Spirit made this being with great care. It was the Bowhead Whale. It was, indeed, the most beautiful and the finest of the things made by the Great Spirit. As it swam, it flowed through the ocean. It sang as it went, and it was in perfect balance with everything around it.

But the Great Spirit saw something else. He saw that the Inupiaq people needed the Bowhead Whale. Without the whale, it would be hard for them to survive. They needed its bones to help build their homes. They needed every part of the great whale.

So the Great Spirit gave the Bowhead to the Inupiaq. He gave them a way to hunt it from their boats covered with walrus hide. He made a special time each spring, when the ice of the ocean would break apart to form a road where the whales would swim. In that whale road, the Open Lead, the whales would come to the surface and wait there to be struck by the harpoons of the Inupiaq. They would continue to do so every year as long as the Inupiaq showed respect to the Bowhead, as long as the Inupiaq only took the few whales that they needed in order to survive.

But the Great Spirit decided this also. At that time each year when the Open Lead formed, when the whale came to the surface to be hunted, the Great Spirit made it so that a heavy cloud of thick mist would hang just above the ice, just above the heads of the whales and the Inupiaq. That thick mist would hang there between the sea and the sky. "Though I give you permission to kill my most perfect creation," the Great Spirit said, "I do not wish to watch it."

—Michael J. Caduto and Joseph Bruchac, *Keepers of the Animals: Native American Stories and Wildlife Activities for Children* (1991)

Above: *A Kwakwaka'wakw (Kwakiutl) ceremonial haroon, Fort Rupert (Tsaxis). This harpoon was used in marriage transfer ceremonies to spear copper as if it were a whale.*
Left: *Detail of the harpoon's tip. (Courtesy of the Collection of the University of British Columbia Museum of Anthropology, cat. no. A3630)*

To survive in the harsh climates in which they lived, coastal Arctic peoples utilized all parts of the whales they caught. They ate the skin, blubber, and meat. They used the gut for waterproof clothing and translucent windows. They dried and inflated the stomachs and intestines to use as storage vessels. They used the oil for cooking, heating, and lighting. Baleen was used as thread and to make whaling gear, fishing equipment, combs, toys, traps, and amulets. The bones were recycled as fences and sled runners, and used in the construction of dwellings, as in this ancient village at Cape Deshney in the Russian Arctic. (Photograph © Robert E. Barber)

mass of blood vessels used by the whale to release heat to control its body temperature. After a hunter had struck a whale, he returned to a hut that had been specially built, where he stayed for three days without food, drink, or the company of women; there he waited for the whale to die and be washed up on shore. To prevent the wounded whale from leaving the area, he would snort occasionally in imitation of a wounded whale. On the fourth day, he bathed in the sea, beating the water with his hands and calling out. He then went to see if the dead whale had washed up on the shore yet. If there was still no sign of the whale, he continued the washing ritual until the dead whale appeared.

Over the centuries, whales have remained part of the fabric of the lives of coastal peoples in the North. In 1986 Patrick Attungana, spokesperson for the Inupiaq, explained to the Alaskan Whaling Commission the relationship between the Inupiaq and the migrating bowheads on which their culture depended:

> We eat the animals of the seas. We eat the animals of the land. We have two sources for our subsistence, we who live on the shores. . . . When the whales travel, they know about St. Lawrence Island, so when they reach there, one of them stop, like they are camping, allowing themselves to be killed. . . . As they keep on traveling, when they reach Barrow, one of them camp[s], caught by the whalers. . . . When the whale is caught, the whale being or spirit never dies. . . . The whole whale gives itself to all people. [When the whales begin migrating south again] the dead whale's being or spirit return to the live whales. The returning whales begin to listen to the whale that had been like camping. He tells them that his hosts were good, the married couple were good to it. . . . The whale that had good hosts starts wishing and telling others that it will camp again the following year. The other whale who did not have good hosts says that it will not camp again. . . . When you hunt in harmony, you don't have problems catching the animals.

The Inuit of the Thule culture migrated from Alaska across the Canadian Arctic over one thousand years ago. They used the bones of the whales they hunted to support the roofs of their winter homes. This structure in Resolute Bay dates from A.D. 1400. By 1650, the climate had cooled and whales no longer visited these shores. The Inuit remained, turning to seals instead of whales as the staple of their diet. (Photograph © Tom Lebovsky)

LEVIATHAN

In coastal Aboriginal cultures, whales were viewed as integral parts of the cultures' self-sustaining circle of life; for other cultures, whales were viewed as terrifying creatures that people only came across when they ventured into the unknown. This account of a whale encounter by an officer in Alexander the Great's army, recorded by Arrian, describes the fear evoked in early sailors who unexpectedly came across whales. The incident took place in the Indian Ocean in the fourth century B.C.:

> As we set sail we observed that in the sea to the east of us water was blown aloft, as happens with a strong whirlwind.

We were terrified and asked our pilots what it was and whence it came. They replied that it was caused by whales, which inhabit this sea. Our sailors were so horrified that the oars fell from their hands.

When Roman scholar Pliny the Elder included whales in his thirty-seven-volume *Historia Naturalis* in A.D. 79, he described them as "a mighty masse and lumpe of flesh without all fashion, armed with most terrible, sharpe, and cutting teeth." He also wrote, "The Indian Sea breedeth the most and the biggest fishes that are: among which the Whales and Whirlpooles called Balaena, take up as much in length as four acres or arpens of land."

Medieval sailors believed that when a whale dived it created a vortex that could swallow a boat, and that the spray from a whale's blow would strip the flesh from any living being it settled on. Early maps showed unknown oceans filled with weird and fanciful creatures with elaborate horns and fearsome teeth gushing waterspouts into the air. Early sailors were extremely wary of whales. One account, recorded in the 1863 text *Chambers Books of Days: A Miscellany of Popular Antiquities*, tells of a Portuguese ship on its way to Brazil that fell becalmed close to a large whale: "The mariners, terrified by the uncouth gambols of the monster, improvised a summary process, and duly exorcised the dreaded cetacean, which, to their great relief, immediately sank to the lowest depths of the ocean." Lucian's *The True History, Book 1* contains a similar report: "Scarcely had we proceeded two days on the sea, when about sunrise a great many Whales and other monsters of the sea, appeared. Among the former, one was of a most monstrous size. This came towards us, open-mouthed, raising the waves on all sides, and beating the sea before him into a foam."

Encounters with unknown creatures, likely whales, were woven into Greek, Roman, and Hebrew mythology. Although there are no longer humpbacks in the Mediterranean, the siren songs heard by Odysseus were most probably the songs of humpback whales transmitted from the depths through the wooden hull of his boat. In Hebrew lore, Leviathan was a sea monster of enormous proportions. Its eyes lit up the sea by night and water boiled from its poisonous hot breath. When God slew the female to prevent the Leviathans breeding and destroying the world, he clothed Adam and Eve in her skin.

Aristotle made a number of accurate observations about whales as early as 350 B.C., including the fact that, even though they lived in the oceans, whales and dolphins breathe air and bear live young, "The dolphin, the whale and all the rest of the cetacea, all, that is to say, that are provided with a blow-hole instead of gills, are viviparous." However, few others had any understanding of the animals and general knowledge of whales remained sketchy for quite some time.

The narrative of Irish monk and traveler Saint Brendan illustrates some of the fanciful stories circulating about whales. In the sixth century, Saint Brendan set sail in an oxhide boat with a company of monks to find the Promised Land. Some believed he sailed as far as Newfoundland

From this view of a fin whale, it is easy to see how sailors of previous centuries might have mistaken this whale for a giant sea serpent. (Photograph © Francois Gohier)

before returning home. During the course of his journey, which is said to have lasted forty years, he and his monks visited a number of remarkable islands.

One island they came upon was stony and barren. As the monks drew their boat up onto the shore, they noticed a few pieces of driftwood but no sand. They spent the night on the island praying while Saint Brendan stayed in the boat. In the morning, Saint Brendan ordered the monks on shore to sing mass, which they did; he joined them in their devotions from the boat deck. When they had finished the mass, they gathered driftwood to light a fire so they could salt the raw meat they were carrying. They collected a pot and the meat from the boat and built a roaring fire on the shore.

As the pot began to boil, the island began to move. The terrified monks abandoned their pot and rushed back to the boat, where Saint Brendan was waiting to help them on board. As they sailed away, the island began to move in the opposite direction. When it was about two miles away, they could still see the flames from their fire burning on its shore. Then Saint Brendan revealed to them the true nature of the "island":

Two monsters representing a baleen whale and a killer whale from the Carta Marina *of Swedish archbishop Olaus Magnus, 1539. Both whales are depicted as having long, sharp teeth.*

> "Brothers, are you surprised at what this island has done?"
> They said: "We are very surprised and indeed terror-stricken."
> He said to them: "My sons, do not be afraid. God revealed to me during the night in a vision the secret of this affair. Where we were was not an island, but a fish—the foremost of all that swim in the ocean. He is always trying to bring his tail to meet his head, but he cannot because of his length. His name is Jasconius."

Later in the voyage, the monks became accustomed to occasional visits from the whale, and one year they even celebrated Easter mass on the creature's enormous back.

In the Arabian tales of *The Book of The Thousand and One Nights*, Scheherazade, the wife of King Schahriar, relates a similar adventure experienced by Sinbad the Sailor:

> One day, after some weeks of sailing out of sight of land, we saw an island in the sea with such fair greenery that it appeared like one of the gardens of Eden. At once the captain made towards this delectable land and, when the anchor had been cast and the ladder lowered, allowed his passengers to disembark.
> All of us merchants landed, carrying food and cooking utensils with us. Some lit fires and prepared a meal, others washed their linen, and others again contented themselves with resting or walking. I was among the last and, without

A drawing based on an engraving from 1621 showing the sixth-century Irish monk St. Brendan the Navigator and his traveling companions celebrating mass on the back of a whale on their journey to the Promised Land. (Courtesy of The Mariners' Museum, Newport News, Virginia)

op in aquis z in mari viuunt. ut foce. cocodrilli ypota
mi. h̄. est equi fluctuales. ✝ DE BALENA.

Est belua in mari q̄ grece aspido delone dr̄. latine si
aspido testudo. Cete z dicta. ob immanitatem cor
poris. ē enim sic ille qui excepit ionam. cuius aluus

neglecting either food or drink, found time to wander among the trees and take pleasure in the strange vegetation.

We were all occupied in these various ways, when the island suddenly shook throughout its length so violently that we were thrown to the ground. While we lay dazed, we saw the captain appear in the bows of his ship and heard him cry in an agonized voice with wild gesturings: "Save yourselves! Come aboard for your lives! That is no island but a gigantic whale! She has lived in the middle of this sea since time was young, and the trees have grown in the sea sand upon her back. You have troubled her repose by lighting fires upon her; now she is moving! Come aboard for your lives, before she sinks in the water and destroys you all!"

Hearing these cries of the captain, the merchants left all they had of clothes, cooking pots and ovens, and rushed towards the ship, which was already weighing anchor. Some of them reached her in time, others did not; for the whale, after bounding terrifically two or three times, sank like lead in the water and involved those who were still upon her back beneath monstrous waves.

Other early tales about whales that verge on the fantastic include the Biblical account of Jonah being swallowed by a whale, in which Jonah survives the ordeal and is returned to land after three days in the whale's stomach: "At the Lord's bidding, a great sea-beast had swallowed him up; and there, in the belly of it, three days spent he and three nights. . . . And now, at the Lord's bidding, the sea-beast cast Jonas up again, high and dry on the beach."

Jonah-like tales can be found in other cultures as well. A Hawaiian legend tells of Makua, a pious widower who lived with his son. Two gods came to visit Makua in disguise and were impressed by his piety and his hospitality. The gods first rewarded Makua with gifts and then decided to test his piety by saying that his son had broken an eating tapu of the gods. Makua loved his son very much but decided that he had no choice but to kill the boy. The gods decided he was indeed a very pious man, and they stayed Makua's hand by sending a great fish to him. Makua saw the fish and climbed onto its back. As he prepared to dive from the fish's back, the fish swallowed him and took him away to a hidden land of the gods. In this land, no one was allowed to weep. The gods sent Makua a vision of his son being forced into the sea by his wife, where he was eaten by a shark. Makua wept when he thought his son was dead, and he was sent home by the gods in the belly of the fish, who deposited him on the shore, where his son came to greet him.

The Celtic tale of Fair, Brown, and Trembling is another story in which whales are capable of swallowing people and then spitting them out again in good condition. A Celtic king had three daughters, Fair, Brown, and Trembling. After a Cinderella-like prelude in which a prince married Trembling when he discovered that she was the owner of a lost slipper, a whale makes an appearance in the story.

This illumination of sailors mistaking the back of a whale for an island dates from twelfth-century England. The mistake seems to have been easily made. In the second century, the Greek Physiologus wrote: "There is a certain whale in the sea called the aspidoceleon, that is exceedingly large like an island. . . . Ignorant sailors tie their ships to the beast as to an island and plant their anchors and stakes in it. They light their cooking fires on the whale, but when it feels the heat it urinates and plunges into the depths, sinking all the ships." (Courtesy of the Bodleian Library, University of Oxford, MS. Ashmole 1511, fol. 86v miniature)

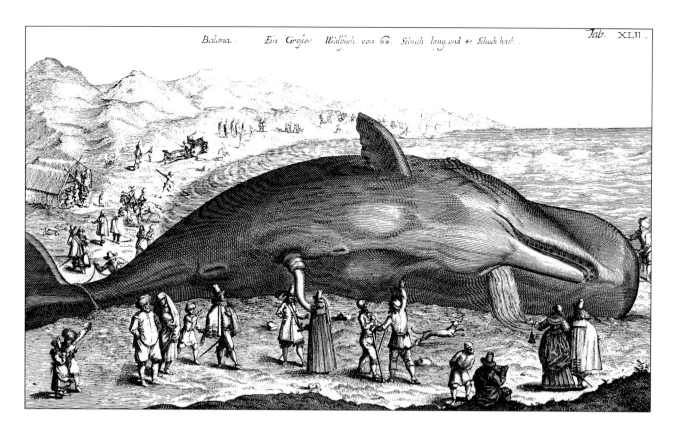

This sperm whale was stranded on a beach at Katwijk, Holland, in 1598. The curious came to gawk at the ungainly-looking monster, unaware of how magnificently it was adapted to its natural environment. From Joanne Jonstonus, Historiae Naturalis *(1649).*

When Trembling gave birth to her first child, she sent for the aide of her sister, Fair. Fair was jealous of her sister and as they were walking along the shore, she pushed Trembling into the sea and a whale swallowed her. Fair went back to the prince and pretended that she was Trembling, but the prince saw through her deception. The next day a young cowherd saw the whale throw Trembling onto the beach. Trembling implored the cowherd to go to the prince to let him know what had happened as the whale would swallow her again with the coming of the next tide. She said that the whale would throw her out and swallow her again three times. She was under the whale's enchantment and could not escape from the beach by herself. If the whale swallowed her a fourth time, she would be lost forever. To free his wife, the prince had to shoot the whale with a silver bullet in the reddish brown spot under its breast fin.

Although Fair gave the cowherd a potion to make him forget his message, on the third day he remembered and the prince saved his wife. In time the prince and Trembling had a daughter, and when she grew up, the little princess married the cowherd who had saved her mother's life.

In Europe, stranded whales were not seen as gifts of food and useful materials from the gods, but as curiosities. People came to stare at the rotting carcasses of the massive sea creatures. Then in the twelfth century, Europeans figured out how to profit from dead whales. As whales slipped from the realms of legend and the heavens into the realm of commerce, their systematic destruction at the hands of humankind began.

This drawing from an engraving by Antoine Wierx shows Jonah being cast out by the whale. (Courtesy of The Mariners' Museum, Newport News, Virginia)

Part Three

OF WHALES
AND MEN

The Nootka claim that the whale allows his death,
To spare people from hunger,
And that therefore they must be worthy of it.
But other men have elected to view the whale
As an essential component of an expanding economy.

—Heathcote Williams, *Whale Nation*

Left: *The discovery of whales in the Arctic Seas sent European nations into an acquisitive frenzy. In 1697, the superintendent of the Dutch whale fishery described "a richly laden fleet . . . comprising 121 Hollanders, whose cargoes consisted of 1252 whales; 54 Hamburghers with 515 whales, 15 Bremeners with 119 whales, and 2 Embdeners with 2 whales: in all which fleet, there was not one clean ship." (Courtesy of the Kendall Whaling Museum, Sharon, Massachusetts, USA)*
Inset: *By the nineteenth century, signing aboard a whaleship was being promoted as a ticket to adventure.*

UNTOLD RICHES

Scandinavians likely encountered whales on their long voyages to North America in the late 900s A.D. Icelandic sagas tell of whales being driven into the fjords to be slaughtered, and by the ninth century, Norwegians were catching whales off the Tromsø coast.

It seems, however, that the first to indulge in commercial whaling were the Basques, who by A.D. 1100 were systematically hunting whales in the Bay of Biscay in northern Spain. By the 1400s, the Basques were expanding their range from the Bay of Biscay across the North Atlantic to the eastern shores of North America. It is likely that, like the Norsemen before them, Basque whalers were familiar with Newfoundland and Labrador prior to the arrival of John Cabot in 1497. Red Bay, Labrador, a Basque whaling station, has been dated at approximately 1536.

In the late sixteenth and early seventeenth centuries, as the Basques continued to pursue whales off the North American coast, Dutch and British merchant ships were searching for a trade route via the northern oceans to the riches of the Orient. Instead they discovered that the frozen archipelago of Spitsbergen north of Norway was a haven for whales. The British and the Dutch wasted no time recruiting experienced Basques to instruct them in the art of whaling.

As whale stocks close to shore were depleted, the whalers moved out onto the high seas. Nineteenth-century British whaling captain William Scoresby described the atmosphere surrounding the Arctic hunt:

> The Providence of God is manifested in the tameness and timidity of many of the largest inhabitants of the earth and sea, whereby they fall victims to the prowess of man, and are rendered subservient to his convenience in life. . . .
>
> Whenever a whale lies on the surface of the water, unconscious of the approach of its enemies, the hardy fisher rows directly upon it; and an instant before the boat touches it, buries his harpoon in its back. . . . The wounded whale, in the surprise and agony of the moment, makes a convulsive effort to escape. Then is the moment of danger. The boat is subjected to the most violent blows from its head, or its fins, but particularly from its ponderous tail which sometimes sweeps the air with such tremendous fury, that both boat and men are exposed to one common destruction. . . .
>
> The first efforts of a "fast-fish," or whale that has been struck, is to escape from the boat, by sinking under water. . . .
>
> A whale, struck near the edge of any large sheet of ice, and passing underneath it, will sometimes run the whole of the lines out of one boat, in the space of eight or ten minutes of time. . . . To retard, therefore, as much as possible, the flight of the whale, it is usual for the harpooner, who strikes it, to cast one, two, or more turns of the line round a kind of post called a bollard; which is fixed within ten or twelve inches of the stem of the boat, for the purpose. Such is the friction of the line, when running round the bollard, that it frequently

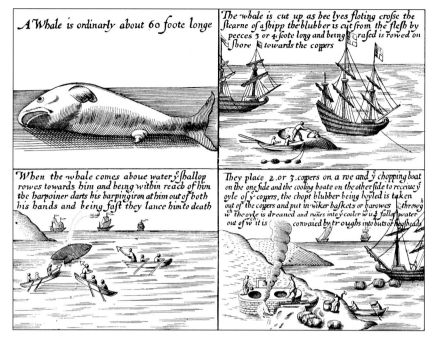

A Whale is ordinarly about 60 foote longe

The whale is cut up as hee lyes floting crosse the stearne of a shipp the blubber is cut from the flesh by peeces 3 or 4 foote long and being rased is rowed on shore towards the coppers

When the whale comes aboue water y shallop rowes towards him and being within reach of him the harpoiner darts his harpingiron at him out of both his hands and being fast they lance him to death

They place 2 or 3 coppers on a rve and y chopping boat on the one side and the cooling boate on the other side to receiue y oyle of y coppers, the chopt blubber being boyled is taken out of the coppers and put in wiker baskets or barowes throwg w the oyle is dreaned and runes into y cooler w u falle water out of w it is convaied by troughs into buts or hogsheads

When the whale is killed hee is in this mann towed to the shipps by twoe or three shal-lops made fast one to another.

Thus they make cleane and scrape y whale fins

The peeces of blubber are towed to the shore side by a shallop and drawne onshore by a crane or caried by twoe menn on a barrowe to y twoe cutters w cutts them the breadth of a trencher and very thine & by twoe boys are caried w handhooks to y choppers

A tent and Coopers at worke

Whales were so plentiful around Spitzbergen, a frozen archipelago north of Norway, that in 1617, the Dutch built permanent furnaces on one of the islands at a place called Smeerenburg or "Blubber Town." By the 1620s, the shore station boasted a summertime population of over a thousand, making it the world's northernmost town. By 1671, whale stocks close to shore had been depleted and Smeerenburg was no more. This sequence depicting the processing of Arctic whales was engraved in 1611, six years before Smeerenburg was established.

envelopes the harpooner in smoke; and if the wood were not repeatedly wetted, would probably set fire to the boat. . . .

Immediately that [the whale] re-appears, the assisting boats make for the place with their utmost speed, and as they reach it, each harpooner plunges his harpoon into its back, to the amount of three, four, or more, according to the size of the whale, and the nature of the situation. Most frequently, however, it descends for a few minutes after receiving the second harpoon, and obliges the other boats to await its return to the surface, before any further attack can be made. It is afterwards actively plied with lances, which are thrust into its body, aiming at its vitals. At length, when exhausted by numerous wounds and the loss of blood, which flows from the huge animal in copious streams, it indicates the approach of its dissolution, by discharging from its "blow-holes," a mixture of blood along with the air and mucus which it usually expires, and finally jets of blood alone. The sea, to a great extent around, is dyed with its blood, and the ice, boats, and men, are sometimes drenched with the same. Its track is likewise marked by a broad pellicle of oil, which exudes from its wounds, and appears on the surface of the sea. Its final capture is sometimes preceded by a convulsive and energetic struggle, in which its tail, reared, whirled, and violently jerked in the air, resounds to the distance of miles. In dying, it turns on its back or on its side; which joyful circumstance is announced by the capturers with the striking of their flags, accompanied with three lively huzzas!

While the Dutch and the British were plundering Arctic waters, the American whale fishery was taking a different turn. In 1620, pilgrims aboard the *Mayflower* traveling from Europe to colonies in the New World had sighted an abundance of whales off the east coast of North America. Their leader, William Bradford, wrote, "And every day we saw whales playing hard by us; of which in that place if we had instruments and means to take them we might make a very rich return." Indeed, the whales were one reason the pilgrims—who had originally been bound for Virginia—decided to alight at Cape Cod and eventually settled the town of Plymouth on the cape's inhospitable western shore.

By the 1640s, the settlers, aided by local Nauset Indians, were shore whaling for right whales. In 1659, a group of Quakers left the main Plymouth colony for the island of Nantucket, where they raised sheep. It was a tenuous existence and the Nantucketers desperately needed other sources of income if their colony was to survive. In 1712, a gale blew Captain Christopher Hussey out to sea, where he killed a strange type of whale and towed it back to Nantucket. On that day the Yankee sperm whale fishery was born.

Less than fifty years after the discovery of that first sperm whale, stocks of sperm whales within a couple of days sailing of the New England coast had been depleted. The whaleships now needed to travel

In 1607, on a failed attempt to sail to the North Pole, the English navigator Henry Hudson reported sighting whales in Arctic waters. The British and the Dutch lost no time in recruiting experienced Basque whalers to teach them how to hunt bowheads. By the end of the century, the Dutch owned 70 percent of all the whaling ships in the Arctic and were flooding Europe with whale oil and baleen. "Dutch Whaling Scene," 1645, by the artist Bonaventura Peeters. (Courtesy of The Mariners' Museum, Newport News, Virginia)

farther afield—something they could not do if they continued the Arctic whalers' style of packing blubber in barrels to ship to their home ports. The mild weather encountered by the Yankee sperm whalers allowed the packed blubber to stay fresh for only a day or two. The solution was to move the tryworks, or boilers, aboard ship and render the whale blubber into oil while the ships were at sea. Fires blazed long into the night and, as the fishery expanded, the stench produced by Yankee whalers rode the ocean breezes to the Azores, the west coast of Africa, the Falkland Islands, Brazil, and Argentina.

Sperm whaling was immortalized in Herman Melville's classic novel *Moby-Dick*, published in 1851. By this time the sperm whalers had rounded Cape Horn and were plying their trade in the Pacific. Melville based aspects of his story on events reported at the time. One of these was the story of the *Essex*, a whaling ship that had been stove by a bull sperm whale in the mid-Pacific in November 1820. This extract, from David Day's 1987 book *The Whale War*, describes the whale's attack on the *Essex* after the ship's whaleboats struck three of the whales in its group. One of the boats had been dealt a severe blow by a harpooned whale and had returned to the *Essex* for repairs. Thomas Nickerson, a cabin boy, describes what happened next:

Sperm whales are found mainly in tropical waters, possibly making the lives of the men who pursued them more enjoyable than the lives of those who pursued whales in the Arctic and Antarctic regions. The voyages were long, however, sometimes lasting a year or more, and life on board the ship could become monotonous when there were no whales in sight. A sailor on the American whaleship Ceres *kept and embellished this daily journal of his 1837 voyage. (Courtesy of The Mariners' Museum, Newport News, Virginia)*

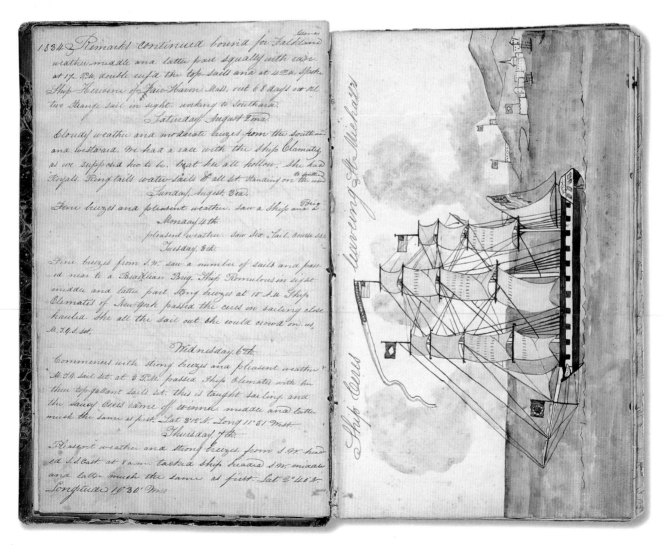

The reason American whalers could travel so far afield was that they processed the whales they caught on board their ships. Unwanted scraps from the whales provided the fuel to heat the huge trypots in which the whales' blubber was rendered into oil. This striking scene of trypots burning into the night was captured by the American marine artist William Edward Norton (1843–1916). (Courtesy of the Kendall Whaling Museum, Sharon, Massachusetts, USA)

I being then at the helm and looking on the windward side of the ship saw a very large whale approaching us. I called out to the mate to inform him of it. On his seeing the whale he instantly gave me an order to put the helm hard up. I had scarcely time to obey the order when I heard a loud cry from several voices at once, that the whale was coming foul of the ship. Scarcely had the sound of their voices reached my ears when it was followed by a tremendous crash, the whale had struck the ship with his head under the larboard fore chains at the water's edge with such force as to shock every man upon his feet. The whale then getting under the ship's bottom came up under the starboard quarters. . . . The monster took a turn off about 300 yards ahead, then turning short came around with his utmost speed and again struck the ship a tremendous blow with his head and with such force as to stove in the whole bow at the water's edge. One of the men who was below at the time came running up on deck saying "The ship is filling with water." We turned our attention to getting clear the boat, the only boat left with us, with which we could expect to escape.

In his 1981 book *Stove by a Whale: Owen Chase and the Essex*, Thomas Heffernan recounts the story of Owen Chase, the first mate of the *Essex* and the author of the most famous account of her sinking. In this passage, Chase considers what might have prompted the sperm whale that sunk his ship to such vengeful action:

> After several hours of idle sorrow and repining I began to reflect upon the accident, and endeavoured to realize by what unaccountable destiny or design . . . this sudden and most deadly attack had been made upon us: by an animal, too, never before suspected of premeditated violence, and proverbial for its insensibility and inoffensiveness. Every fact seemed to warrant me in concluding that it was any thing but chance which directed his operations; he made two several attacks upon the ship, at a short interval between them, both of which, according to their direction, were calculated to do us the most injury, by being made ahead, and thereby combining the speed of the two objects for the shock; to effect which, the exact manoeuvres which he made were necessary. His aspect was most horrible, and such as indicated resentment and fury. He came directly from the shoal which we had just before entered, and in which we had struck three of his companions, as if fired with revenge for their sufferings.

In creating the rogue whale Moby Dick, Melville also included characteristics ascribed to Mocha Dick, a huge white bull sperm whale who from 1810 to 1859 terrorized whalers in the Pacific, killing at least thirty men in the process. Melville wrote of his fictional whale:

> [T]here was enough in the earthly make and incontestable character of the monster to strike the imagination with

The oil that resulted from boiling down whale blubber was used for such things as lighting, the manufacture of soap and paint, and the processing of wool and leather. (Courtesy of Old Dartmouth Historical Society–New Bedford Whaling Museum)

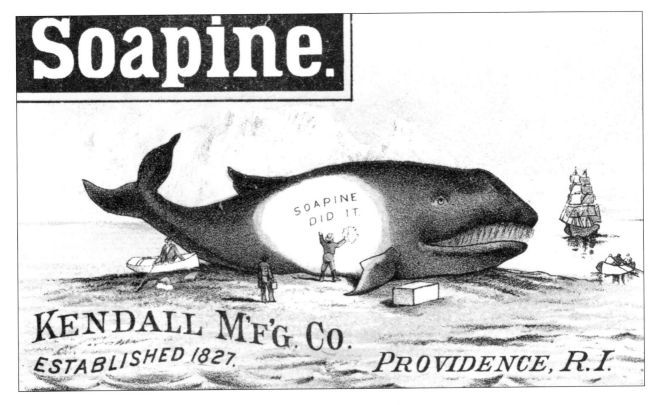

USES FOR A SPERM WHALE

"In memory I stand again on a slippery whaling platform in Alaska watching a workman with a razor knife as long as his arm stab cleanly through the flesh of a sperm whale's head and let the spermaceti flow. Minute after minute and barrel after barrel it gushed clean and unpolluted, as clear as water, bubbling and trickling. Then a filmy haze formed on the surface; the oily liquid cooled; ropy strings emerged—icicles, frozen waterfalls."

—Victor B. Sheffer, *The Year of the Whale*

Ambergris, a digestive byproduct of the sperm whale, used to be worth its weight in gold. In a paper read before the Royal Society in 1783, a Dr. Schwediawer reported on the possible medicinal properties of ambergris: "A sailor . . . who had the curiosity to try the effects of some recent ambergris upon himself, took half an ounce of it melted upon the fire, and found it a good purgative." *Brande's Manual of Chemistry* listed other uses: "In Asia and part of Africa, ambergris is not only used as a medicine and perfume, but considerable use is also made of it in cooking, by adding it to several dishes as a spice. A great quantity of it is also constantly bought by the pilgrims who travel to Mecca, probably to offer it there, and make use of it in fumigations, in the same manner as frankincense is used in Catholic countries. The Turks make use of it as an aphrodisiac. Our perfumers add it to scented pastiles, candles, balls, bottles, gloves, and hair powder; and its essence is mixed with pomatum for the face and hands, either alone or united with musk."

Spermaceti oil was highly prized. It was used in cosmetics, pharmaceuticals, biodegradable detergents, greases, printing inks, wetting agents, fatty alcohols, fatty acids, as an additive for heavy-duty lubricating oils, as a chemical intermediate, and for processing leather. The oil burns with a bright, smokeless flame, and American railroads used it in signal lamps until the end of the World War I. It was considered the finest oil for the lubrication of delicate machinery and for breaking in internal combustion engines, because it maintains its viscosity over a wide range of temperatures. Until the early 1980s, it was used in the U.S. space

program and upper end car engines such as Rolls Royce. As a wax, it was used to make smokeless candles and to waterproof the feet of soldiers in trenches in the World War I.

The internal organs of sperm whales have yielded much of use to the pharmaceutical industry. The liver is good source of vitamins and contains as much carotene as fifty tons of carrots. The pancreas yields a substance to make insulin. The pituitary gland yields an adrenocorticotropic substance for the treatment of arthritis and gout. The collagen in the flukes was used to make surgical sponges as temporary replacements for donor skin in the treatment of burns.

Although sperm whale meat is dark and mostly unpalatable, some cuts fetched high prices in the Japanese whale meat market. The rest was used for the production of feed meal for animals. The stock after fat extraction was used to make gelatin. The tendons were used in the manufacture of glue. The Soviets tanned the skin to make shoe soles and work gloves.

The spermaceti oil in the sperm whale's bulbous head was especially prized as a lubricant for delicate machinery. This advertisement offers consumers the opportunity to experience some of the thrills of the chase. (Courtesy of Old Dartmouth Historical Society–New Bedford Whaling Museum)

unwonted power. For, it was not so much his uncommon bulk that so much distinguished him from other sperm whales, but, as was elsewhere thrown out—a peculiar snow-white wrinkled forehead, and a high, pyramidical white hump. There were his prominent features; the tokens whereby, even in the limitless, uncharted seas, he revealed his identity, at a long distance, to those who knew him.

The rest of his body was so streaked, and spotted, and marbled with the same shrouded hue, that, in the end, he had gained his distinctive appellation of the White Whale; a name, indeed, literally justified by his vivid aspect, when seen gliding at high noon through a dark blue sea, leaving a milky-way wake of creamy foam, all spangled with golden gleamings.

By 1840, Yankee sperm whaling had reached its peak. As women's fashions changed, there was a shift from hunting sperm whales for their oil to hunting baleen whales for their baleen. The sperm whale fishery took an additional hit in 1859, when the discovery of petroleum in Pennsylvania led to a drastic decline in the demand for animal oil.

In 1858, American whaler Charles Scammon found the breeding places of the Pacific gray whale—shallow, protected waters off the coast of Mexico where they gathered in large numbers and were vulnerable to attack. Although Scammon's whalers were armed with the latest in whaling technology—a bomb lance had been invented in 1850—their first attempts at hunting gray whales in the breeding lagoons was little short of disastrous. Gray whales under attack, it seemed, turned quite nasty. In his 1874 book *The Marine Mammals of the Northwestern Coast of North America,* Scammon describes his encounter with the grays:

> Early the next morning, the boats were again in eager pursuit; but before the animal was struck, it gave a dash with its flukes, staving the boat into fragments, and sending the crew in all directions. One man had his leg broken, another had an arm fractured, and three others were more or less injured—the officer of the boat being the only one who escaped unharmed. The relief boat, while rescuing the wounded men, was also staved by a passing whale, leaving only one boat afloat. The tender being near at hand, however, a boat from that vessel rendered assistance, and all returned to the brig. When the first boat arrived with her freight of crippled passengers, it could only be compared to a floating ambulance crowded with men—the uninjured supporting the helpless.

Once the technique of using the bomb lance had been perfected, the killing of the Pacific gray whale was pursued with renewed vigor. With obvious relish, Scammon describes this frantic scene:

Before the invention of plastic and the discovery of petroleum, whalebone or baleen and whale oil were used for many different purposes. (Courtesy of The Mariners' Museum, Newport News, Virginia)

[In the headwaters of the Main Lagoon] the objects of pursuit were found in large numbers, and here the scene of slaughter was exceedingly picturesque and unusually exciting, especially on a calm morning, when the mirage would transform not only the boats and their crews into fantastic imagery, but the whales, as they sent forth their towering spouts of aqueous vapour, frequently tinted with blood, would appear greatly distorted. At one time, the upper sections of the boats, with their crews, would be seen gliding over the molten-looking surface of the water, with a portion of the colossal form of the whale appearing for an instant, like a spectre, in the advance; or both boats and whales would assume ever-changing forms, while the report of the bomb guns would sound like the sudden discharge of musketry; but one can not fully realize, unless he be an eye-witness, the intense and boisterous excitement of the reckless pursuit, by a large fleet of boats from different ships, engaged in a morning's whaling foray. Numbers of them will be fast to whales at the same time, and the stricken animals, in their efforts to escape, can be seen darting in every direction through the water, or breaching headlong clear of its surface, coming down with a splash that sends columns of foam in every direction, and with a rattling report that can be heard beyond the surrounding shores.

1. Oar. 2. Boat-warf. 3. Boat-hook. 4. Paddle. 5. Boat-sails. 6. Sweeping-line-buoy. 7. Lead to Sweeping-line. 8. Chock-pin. 9. Short-warp. 10. Boat-piggin. 11. Boat-keg. 12. Lantern-key. 13. Sweeping-line. 14. Boat-hatchet. 15. Lance-warp. 16. Boat-grapnel. 17. Boat-knife. 18. Fog-horn. 19. Line-tub. 20. Boat-bucket. 21. Drag. 22. Nipper. 23. Boat-crotch. 24. Boat-compass. 25. Boat-anchor. 26. Row-lock. 27. Tub-oar-crotch. 28. Hand-lance. 29. One-flued-harpoon. 30. Toggle-harpoon. 31. Boat-spade. 32. & 33. Greener's-Gun-harpoon. 34. Greener's Harpoon-gun. 35. Bomb-lance. 36. Bomb-lance gun

Charles M. Scammon, in his treatise on whaling, includes this useful diagram detailing the arsenal available to the whalers of his day: 28. Hand-lance. 29. One flued-harpoon. 30. Toggle harpoon. 31. Boat spade. 32 and 33. Greener's Gun harpoon. 34. Greener's Harpoon-gun. 35. Bomb-lance. 36. Bomb-lance gun.

As the American and European whalers plied their trade on the high seas or along the shores of North America—mainly in search of sperm whales, gray whales, right whales, and bowheads—shore whaling for migrating humpbacks was becoming a profitable venture off the coasts of South Africa and Australia. In one particularly interesting incident, described by Jacqueline Nayman in her 1973 book *Whales, Dolphins, and Man*, the whalers credited killer whales with helping them with their catch:

The most extraordinary story of cooperation between cetaceans and man concerns the killer whale. It comes from Twofold Bay, Australia, which is on the Pacific coast, south of

Sydney, and lies on the route taken by whales on their journey from the summer feeding grounds of the Antarctic, north, to their breeding grounds nearer the Tropics. There was a shore whaling station here between 1866 and 1928 and from this a family of early settlers hunted the migrating humpbacks and minke whales in open boats. In the month of July, when the whale-bone whales arrived, so did a pack of killer whales, which stationed itself at the mouth of the bay. When the killers sighted their quarry they would start "lob-tailing" or "flop-tailing", that is to say, beating their tails on the surface of the water—a noisy practice. This may have been a signal to alert the other killers in the pack, but the whalers took it to be a signal for themselves, and quickly launched their boats. The whale was approached on one side by the boats, and, on the other, by the killers who kept harrying the whale and driving it towards the shore, and this meant that a whale which would normally take up to twelve hours or more to chase and kill could be despatched by the whalers in an hour.

Once the whale was harpooned the killers played their most important part in this grizzly [sic] partnership. Four of them would station themselves under the head of the whale, preventing it from sounding, while the others swam on either side of it, throwing themselves one after another on top of it and covering its blow-hole. The exhausted whale was then killed, and the men attached an anchor to the harpoon line and left it to the killers for a couple of days. This, however, was not entirely altruistic for these whales sink when they die and do not rise again until inflated by gases of putrefaction. The sinking of the whale did not incommode the killers, of course, and they took the tongue and the lips as their share.

There is something very unattractive about the role the killers played in this action. One feels an aversion to their siding with man against one of their own kind, but perhaps this is sentimentality or anthropomorphism. Certainly the men of Twofold Bay did not feel this way. They were fond of their pack of killers, and, when the last of them, Old Tom, died, he was not rendered down for oil; instead his skeleton was carefully cleaned and mounted, and put on show at the nearby town of Eden.

NEW HEIGHTS OF DESTRUCTION

In the last decades of the nineteenth century, the inventions of a Norwegian named Svend Foyn changed the face of whaling. Foyn invented the whalecatcher boat: a sleek steel-hulled vessel powered by steam with a harpoon cannon mounted on its bow, a whale line that absorbed the shock when a whale pulled against it, and a winch to haul the dead whale to the surface. In the 1880s, Foyn added to this arsenal the technique of inflating whale carcasses with compressed air. Thanks to Foyn's

This nineteenth-century engraving shows killer whales attacking a bowhead whale. Charles M. Scammon noted, "The attack of these wolves of the ocean upon their gigantic prey may be likened, in some respects, to a pack of hounds holding the stricken deer at bay. They cluster about the animal's head, some of their number breaching over it, while others seize it by the lips and haul the bleeding monster under water; and when captured, should the mouth be open, they eat out its tongue."

The Yankee whalers stayed at sea until they had filled their holds with barrels and barrels of whale oil. The crew stayed on for the duration of the voyage and were entitled to a meager share of the profits once the journey was over. (Photograph courtesy of Old Dartmouth Historical Society–New Bedford Whaling Museum)

advances in whaling technology, Norwegian whaling companies were soon pursuing rorquals (blues, fins, and seis who had previously escaped the whalers' focused attentions because of their speed and power) across the North Atlantic, and by the end of the century, rorquals swimming close to the coasts of Norway had been fished out.

As the twentieth century dawned, another Norwegian, Carl Anton Larsen, promoted the idea of whaling in Antarctica. South Georgia, discovered by British navigator Captain James Cook in 1775, became the whalers' base because its shores were ice-free year-round. On December 22, 1904, the slaughter began, and South Georgia became the most southerly inhabited spot in the world.

In Antarctica, the whalers had discovered the winter feeding grounds of humpback, blue, fin, and sei whales. The whalers' catches were limited only by the capacity of the land-based whaling stations to process the whales. New uses were being found for whale products as spring steel and plastic were replacing baleen, and petroleum was an abundant and inexpensive substitute for many uses of whale oil. A process called hydrogenation allowed whale oil to be turned into an inoffensive white solid used for the manufacture of margarine. According to business historian Charles Wilson, the process was not widely publicized because, "to look kindly upon blubber as a source of imitation butter called for a more lively appreciation of the wonders of science than the average housewife could muster." Glycerin was a byproduct of the hydrogenation process and during World War I it was in high demand for the manufacture of explosives. The price of whale oil soared.

In 1923, Carl Anton Larsen—finding his activities in the Antarctic constrained by the British, who controlled the licenses for land-based whaling stations—entered the Ross Sea and ushered in the age of pelagic whaling with huge factory ships that no longer needed to return to port to process their cargoes. At first the whales were still butchered in the ocean alongside the factory ships; however, in 1925, with the introduction of the stern slipway, the whales could be hauled aboard for processing. This meant the factory ships no longer had to lie in wait in protected anchorages for the catcher boats to bring the whales to them. They could now accompany the catcher boats out over the high seas. There was nowhere left for the whales to flee. It took five hundred years to destroy stocks of right whales around the world. The sperm whale fishery lasted two hundred years. In contrast, it took less than seventy years to deplete blue whale stocks—possibly beyond the point of recovery.

R. B. Robertson, a senior medical officer on a British Antarctic whaling expedition from 1950 to 1951, describes modern whaling techniques in *Of Whales and Men*, published in 1954:

> The general plan of attack on the cetacean world was this:
> One of our little whalecatching ships, commanded by Thor,
> that phenomenon among gunners, the former New York taxi-
> driver, had gone ahead of us by several days to "look for the

whales." Thor had headed due south to the edge of the pack ice, which he was now skirting in an easterly direction, somewhere south of the South Sandwich Islands. Every few hours he reported back to the factory ship. Accompanying us were the other sixteen small vessels that made up our fleet: catchers, corvettes, and buoy boats. These were ahead, astern, and all round us. "Like a hen and her chickens" is the conventional metaphor for such occasions, but, though our huge ship may have behaved like a lumbering old hen, these vicious little hawklets around us were no chickens. In a day or two they would be biting, and biting hard and fatally, at the greatest of the mammals.

When we reached the whales in any quantity, the thirteen catchers, assisted by their superior speed of fifteen knots, would draw ahead of us and fan out over an arc of ocean that in the beginning would be about fifty miles across. Within this arc, between us and the catchers, would steam the two buoy boats, vessels almost identical with the catchers and armed like them. Their job would be to buoy and collect such whales as the catchers killed, and do a bit of hunting themselves if circumstances permitted. Also in the arc would be the two unarmed corvettes, which would form a fast connecting shuttle service between us and the fleet of small ships, and would tow in to us the dead whales. Communication within the fleet would be by a continuous day-and-night radio-telephone service.

Once whales had been spotted, the catcher boats went out in pursuit. Robertson describes a catcher boat closing in for the kill:

There was no pretense of creeping up on the whale—the thrash of our propeller could be heard by every living thing in the sea for miles around. Thor's aim was to get to the spot before the whale realized what was going on and sounded, or else to scare it into a surface dash to windward and, by means of our two or three knots superiority in speed, to follow it up and come within hitting distance—around fifty to a hundred feet—of the modern harpoon gun.

As we came near shooting range, Thor precipitately left the wheel, which old Angus was ready to grab, and ran down the flying bridge—an elevated walk-way that joins the wheel bridge to the gun platform in the bows. The harpoon gun stood ready. A simple swivel gun, with a pistol grip and a sighting-bar along the top, it was loaded with a six-foot harpoon weighing two hundred pounds. Murderous enough in itself, the harpoon was made more lethal by a grenade attached to its point, fused to explode in three seconds when the harpoon, if the shooting was good, should be lodged in some vital part of the whale's great body. . . .

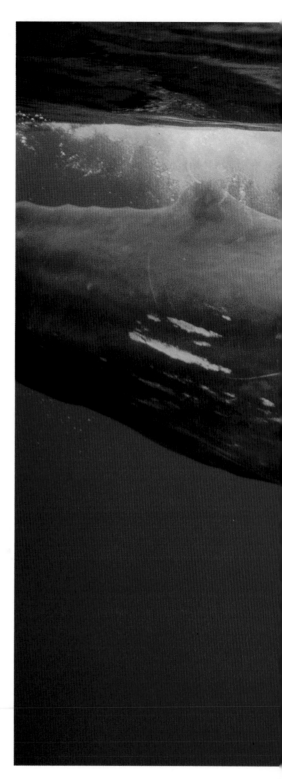

Herman Melville's nineteenth-century classic Moby-Dick tells of a Yankee whaling captain's pursuit of a rogue male sperm whale. Sperm whales continued to be pursued in the oceans of the world until a global moratorium on whaling was imposed in 1986. (Photograph © Francois Gohier)

The Greener's gun was one of the mid-nineteenth-century technological inventions that made the whaler's life easier. A labor-saving device, it launched a harpoon with a greater velocity than could be achieved by throwing it manually. This drawing is from Charles M. Scammon's The Marine Mammals of the Northwestern Coast of North America, *published in 1874.*

Thor swore at the mate. The mate swore back and found time between breaths to curse old Angus at the wheel. . . . The plump engineer down at the winch began to yell profane encouragement to all and sundry. The engine-room telegraph began to yammer as Thor started and stopped his little ship, wheeled it, and sometimes went astern. The cross-talk became even more heated and impious. . . . Then, in the middle of it all, there was the clap of a cannon shot, and it seemed obvious to me, the untutored observer, that Thor had accidentally pulled the trigger in a paroxysm of wrath. But no! There was the whale, which everybody seemed to have forgotten, thrashing the water fifty feet off the bows, with the harpoon securely fixed in a wound just forward of its dorsal fin, and blood gushing into the sea. The dull detonation of the grenade inside the whale ended this stage of the shooting.

Sometimes the whale is killed outright, but more often it either races away on the surface or dives deep as though to think over this disconcerting matter of an explosion inside its tummy. This one was a "sounder," and the nylon rope whirred out of its locker in the bows of our ship as the whale plunged down.

Then began a battle between whale and catcher which can only be understood properly by one who has played a fighting fish on rod and line. The fish in this case is no salmon measured in pounds, however, but has the size and weight of a large Coast Guard cutter. The "hook" has the weight of a plowshare and is twice its size. The "cast" is not a thin strand of gut, but twenty fathoms of three-inch nylon rope that will take a strain of thousands of tons. The "line" is even stouter hempen rope. The "rod" is the mast of the catcher, up which the line runs; it bends and takes an even strain as the angler's rod does to the fighting salmon. And the "reel" at the butt of the rod, taking in line, letting it run, reeling in gently, is a powerful winch. On this winch our fat, cheerful Scottish engineer played the whale, as in his youth he had played the salmon in his native highland rivers. The whale did not stand a chance.

For, unlike a fish, it had to rise to the surface to breathe, and, each time it did so, Thor was waiting, his gun loaded with a "killer" harpoon, which had another grenade on its tip, but no rope attached. The harpoon gun boomed again; there was a welter of blood under our bows and flowing around the ship, and our whale, which did not oblige us with the traditional spout of blood or "chimney afire," as the old whale-men termed it, quietly turned its belly upward and was dead.

By the 1930s, it was becoming increasingly obvious that something needed to be done if the whaling industry was to survive. In 1930, the League of Nations made the first attempt at the international control of whaling. The following year, the Geneva Convention for the Regulation of Whaling forbade countries that subscribed to the convention to kill right whales and females of other species with calves, protected the rights of Aboriginal whalers, and introduced the licensing of whaling vessels. A Bureau of Whaling Statistics was established in Norway. The International Whaling Commission was created in 1946 and additional protection was extended to right whales in 1949.

Despite the various restrictions and regulations put in place, whale stocks continued to decline. Whaling nations decided it was time to learn more about the whales. Perhaps a scientific solution could be found? Whatever the scientists thought, it is clear from contemporary accounts, including R. B. Robertson's, that the men chasing the whales were less than enthusiastic about the scientists' projects:

> I found, during our discussion, that Adamson—the practical though intelligent whaleman—adopted a tolerant but mildly contemptuous attitude toward all whaling research; but on one aspect of it he became scathing and even profane—the researches carried out by the Royal Research Ship Discovery II, the vessel of the Royal Oceanographic Society, which is permanently engaged in investigations in sub-Antarctic waters.
>
> "That damn ship is a waste of public money!" he averred (I think unjustly). "She spends all her time wandering round the edge of the pack ice shooting little silver harpoons about six inches long into all the whales she sights. The harpoons are marked with the date and place the whale was sighted, and the idea is that we recover them and send them back to London, so that they can work out how far and in which direction the whale has traveled between meeting Discovery II and being killed by us. A very fine theory, and there's a reward for sending in the silver markers, although I've never collected it yet. But, if you go down aft there and listen to the blubber-slicing machine, which is exactly the same as a kitchen meat-chopper, you'll hear it humming along, then suddenly snarl and come to a full stop with a broken blade, and we know when that happens it's another of those bluidy Discovery harpoons. And when the repairers have worked for two or three hours extricating it from the blades and getting the machine working again, the market will be a twisted lump of metal, and the date and place engraved on it couldn't be read by a hieroglyphic expert."

Whaling activity reached its zenith in 1960 and then began a steady decline. By the mid-1960s, most nations, with the exception of the Russia and Japan, had ceased whaling on the high seas, although a few, such as Norway, maintained coastal whaling stations. One of the forces keeping whaling alive after 1960 was the sale of whale meat to Japan.

The nineteenth-century Yankee whalers employed essentially the same techniques to hunt whales as the Basques had used in the twelfth century. They set off after whales in small wooden boats and killed them using hand-held harpoons. The "Nantucket sleigh ride" occurred when a whale tried to escape the harpoons embedded in its flesh and ended up dragging the whaleboat attached to the other end of the harpoon lines at speeds of up to twenty-five miles an hour (40 kph). Usually the whale eventually tired and was easily dispatched. Sometimes, however, it was the whaleboat that came to grief, as depicted in this painting "All in a Day's Work" by Charles S. Raleigh, 1878–1880. (Courtesy of Old Dartmouth Historical Society–New Bedford Whaling Museum)

PAUSE FOR THOUGHT

In the 1970s, as whale numbers continued to decline, public attitudes towards whales began to change. Two orcas, Moby Doll and Namu, had been kept in captivity for short periods of time in the early 1960s and helped people see whales as intelligent individuals with lives of their own rather than as an exploitable resource that was there for the taking. People began to actively question the ethics of whaling and to pose questions about what attitudes towards whaling had to say about the values of the human race. Carl Sagan, in his 1973 book *The Cosmic Connection*, had this to say:

> The Cetacea hold an important lesson for us. The lesson is not about whales and dolphins, but about ourselves. There is at least moderately convincing evidence that there is another class of intelligent beings on Earth besides ourselves. They have behaved benignly and in many cases affectionately toward us. We have systematically slaughtered them. There is a monstrous and barbaric traffic in the carcasses and vital fluids of whales. Oil is extracted for lipstick, industrial lubricants and other purposes, even though this makes, at best, marginal economic sense—there are effective substitute lubricants. But why, until recently, has there been so little outcry against this slaughter, so little compassion for the whale?

The possibility of the extinction of animal species had not been considered until 1796, when the issue had been raised by Baron George Cuvier, an expert in paleontology and comparative anatomy. Thereafter, not much thought was given to the idea until the publication of Charles Darwin's *Origin of Species* sixty-three years later. Herman Melville, in *Moby-Dick*, was one of the first to voice the possibility that the world's stocks of whales were not inexhaustible: "The moot point is, whether Leviathan can long endure so wide a chase, and so remorseless a havoc; whether he must not at last be exterminated from the waters, and the last whale, like the last man, smoke his last pipe, and then himself evaporate in the final puff."

By the 1970s, it was apparent that whales really were in danger of disappearing forever. The decade was a time of environmental activism and a call to action before it was too late. Canadian writer Margaret Atwood picked up where Melville's warning left off and gave a new twist to *Moby-Dick* with a short story called "The Afterlife of Ishmael":

> After Ishmael had been rescued and brought ashore, he told the account of his ordeal to the newspapers. The White Whale was a good enough story, and if he exaggerated a little, who was to know? With the proceeds he bought himself a small cottage on a hill overlooking the sea. He set up the jawbone of a whale as a gateway to the little garden where he grew sunflowers and a few vegetables, and at first he was happy enough.

GUESS WHAT'S FOR DINNER?

Although whale meat was popular in Japan, other nations did not find it quite as appealing. A campaign to encourage British housewives to buy whale meat after World War II failed miserably. Partly it was the red color of the whale meat that people found offensive—a color perhaps unexpected from an animal that lives in the sea—or maybe it was just the thought of eating a whale. Whatever the reason, the reaction of F. D. Ommanney's guest at an Antarctic whaling station, recorded in his 1971 book *Lost Leviathan*, sums up many Westerners' attitudes toward whale meat:

> I recall an occasion at South Georgia when an old transport ship flying the Greek flag came into the harbour and lay forlornly at anchor off our jetty awaiting some repair or other. We heard that the skipper was an Englishman and so asked him to dinner. He arrived carefully dressed in his best suit with many creases showing that it had lain in a drawer for a very long time. We had chosen the menu with great care. There was dried lentil soup, fried whale steaks with onions, dehydrated potatoes and tinned mixed vegetable cubes, followed by a choice of pêche Melba, made with tinned peaches and tinned milk, or biscuits and mousetrap [cheese]—a meal fit for a king, we thought.
>
> During the soup we conversed lightheartedly. "I visited the whaling station this morning," our guest said. "What a disgusting sight! They tell me the Norwegians actually eat the meat of whales, but then I suppose the Norwegians will eat anything."
>
> After his second helping of whale meat he said, "What excellent beef steak! How on earth did you manage to get it out here?"
>
> Over the pêche Melba we told him. Our guest turned a pale shade of green and, excusing himself, went outside to lose his entire dinner in the snow.

A Recipe for Whale Steak

That intrepid recorder of whaling in the 1950s, R. B. Robertson, had his own recommendation for cooking whale to impress company:

> Take a ten-pound cut from the rump of a finback whale, just aft of the dorsal fin. (It must be a fin whale or, if you can find one, a humpback. If any New York waiter offers you blue whale, take it in preference to beef, but complain about the absence of fin from the menu; and, if any man tells you he has eaten sperm whale, or that any stomach could tolerate what even the Cape pigeons and the killer whales spurn, give him the lie, even though his name be Melville.) Hang your cut of fin rump steak up on a hook, preferably in a fairly warm spot exposed to the sun. Leave it there for three days. The horrid black mess you will see when you return at the end of that period may put you off whale meat for the rest of your days, but do not be deceived or discouraged. Hold your nose, cut away all the black crust, and bury it deeply far away from your house. In the center of the cut you will find about two pounds of fresh, juicy, oil-free, fatless steak. Put this under a scorching broiler and char it quickly on both sides. Then put it on the table and cut from it the finest pound of medium-rare steak you ever ate in your life.

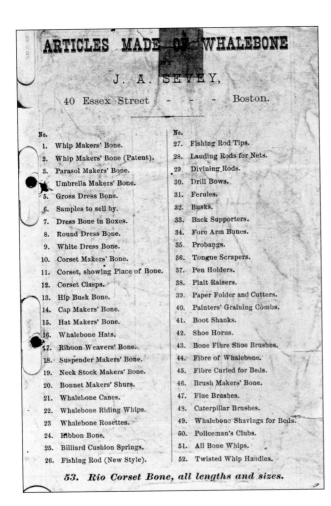

ARTICLES MADE OF WHALEBONE

J. A. SEVEY,

40 Essex Street - - - Boston.

No.		No.	
1.	Whip Makers' Bone.	27.	Fishing Rod Tips.
2.	Whip Makers' Bone (Patent).	28.	Landing Rods for Nets.
3.	Parasol Makers' Bone.	29.	Divining Rods.
4.	Umbrella Makers' Bone.	30.	Drill Bows.
5.	Gross Dress Bone.	31.	Ferules.
6.	Samples to sell by.	32.	Busks.
7.	Dress Bone in Boxes.	33.	Back Supporters.
8.	Round Dress Bone.	34.	Fore Arm Bones.
9.	White Dress Bone.	35.	Probangs.
10.	Corset Makers' Bone.	36.	Tongue Scrapers.
11.	Corset, showing Place of Bone.	37.	Pen Holders.
12.	Corset Clasps.	38.	Plait Raisers.
13.	Hip Busk Bone.	39.	Paper Folder and Cutters.
14.	Cap Makers' Bone.	40.	Painters' Graining Combs.
15.	Hat Makers' Bone.	41.	Boot Shanks.
16.	Whalebone Hats.	42.	Shoe Horns.
17.	Ribbon Weavers' Bone.	43.	Bone Fibre Shoe Brushes.
18.	Suspender Makers' Bone.	44.	Fibre of Whalebone.
19.	Neck Stock Makers' Bone.	45.	Fibre Curled for Beds.
20.	Bonnet Makers' Shurs.	46.	Brush Makers' Bone.
21.	Whalebone Canes.	47.	Flue Brushes.
22.	Whalebone Riding Whips.	48.	Caterpillar Brushes.
23.	Whalebone Rosettes.	49.	Whalebone Shavings for Beds.
24.	Ribbon Bone.	50.	Policeman's Clubs.
25.	Billiard Cushion Springs.	51.	All Bone Whips.
26.	Fishing Rod (New Style).	52.	Twisted Whip Handles.

53. Rio Corset Bone, all lengths and sizes.

Above left: *"Whalebone" does not refer to the bones of a whale but to the long keratinous fringes that hang from the jaws of baleen whales. Baleen is firm yet flexible, making it suited to a wide variety of household uses. The list shown here is fairly comprehensive. In earlier times, baleen was reportedly shredded to make the plumes for knights' helmets. (Courtesy of Old Dartmouth Historical Society– New Bedford Whaling Museum)*

Above right: *For more than two hundred years, the supply of baleen from Arctic whales followed the vagaries of European women's fashion. At the end of the nineteenth century, when fashions finally moved away from hooped skirts and whalebone corsets, the global demand for baleen declined precipitously. (Photograph courtesy of Old Dartmouth Historical Society–New Bedford Whaling Museum)*

When a number of years had passed Ishmael realized that there was nothing for him to do on land. He wanted nobility and danger, he was an addict, and these things could be found only at sea. He went down to the harbour to ship aboard a whaler once more. There are no more whalers, they told him. Not the kind you are suited for. No one stands in a rowboat and throws harpoons at whales any more, no one is that stupid. Now it's all done with radar and guns. It's a harvest, not a hunt. Anyway, what's so noble about dog food?

Disconsolate, Ishmael returned to his cottage. He couldn't understand how a century and a half had passed; he couldn't understand why time had failed to include him. Why wasn't he dead?

That night an angel appeared to him. It manifested itself as an oblong, huge, whitish, like a dirigible balloon, with a small eye on either side. He knew it was an angel because it glowed.

Who are you? he asked in a trembling voice.

I am your judge, said the angel. You have been condemned.

What for? asked Ishmael, with a slight whine, for apart from a few minor lies he didn't think he'd done much that was wrong.

Murder, said the angel.

But I've never killed anyone in my life, said Ishmael. As God is my witness.

Ah, said the angel. Exactly the problem. I was not sent by the God of men but by the God of the whales. Your mistake as well as your crime, was to believe only in the first.

Ishmael, despite his terror, found the notion of a God of the whales so ridiculous that he couldn't help smiling. Well then, what is my sentence? he asked, as if indulging a small child. He had ceased to believe in the angel; he thought he was having a bad dream.

Your sentence has almost been carried out already, said the angel. You are condemned to remain alive forever in a world empty of whales. Your sentence is much worse than that pronounced upon Ahab, because your guilt is greater.

But why? said Ishmael peevishly. I admired the whales, he hated them. Why I am not more innocent than he? I after all did nothing.

Precisely, said the angel.

Not only was there the growing feeling that a world without whales would be a lesser place in which to live, people also began to consider— from a purely practical point of view— that altering the ecology of the earth by removing such important links in the chain of living beings might have disastrous consequences for our own survival. In 1979, in "Why Man Needs the Whales," economic geographer George Small was one of those who raised the alarm:

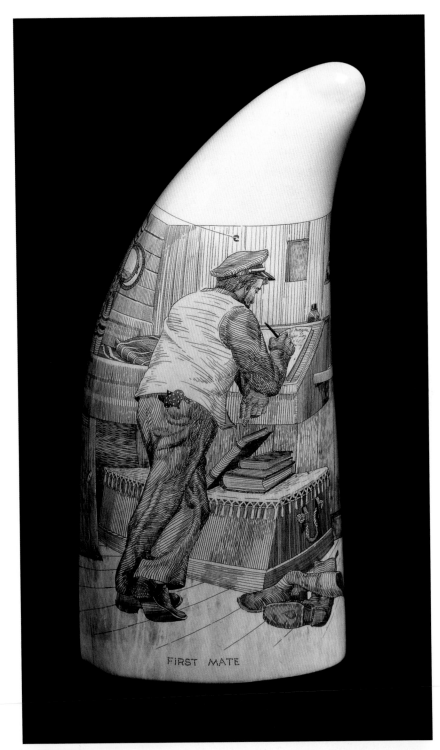

To while away the time at sea, whalers carved the peglike teeth from the bottom jaws of sperm whales in an art known as scrimshaw. The piece "First Mate" is attributed to Francisco Rapoza and dated about 1930. In a pinch baleen could be used for scrimshaw as well. This piece of baleen was fashioned for a corset and likely would not have been for public viewing. Perhaps it was for a loved one to wear close to her heart? (Courtesy of The Mariners' Museum, Newport News, Virginia)

Most of us are raised with the belief that man is the most important and most intelligent animal on earth and that we have a very special relationship with the Creator. We believe we are superior to other animals and have a right, even duty, to subdue and use them for our own benefit. As a species we are not accountable to any other on this, "our" earth. It comes as a surprise and a shock to many of my students when they learn that few animals depend on us, but that we depend on many of them for our continued existence. . . .

Every human being has a biological need that must be constantly met—oxygen. And 70% of the oxygen added to the atmosphere each year comes from plankton in the sea. Serious damage to the world ocean therefore could endanger the entire atmosphere of the earth. During the last two decades man has killed so many of the large whales that four species have been rendered commercially as well as almost biologically extinct. These are the blue whale, the fin whale, the humpback and the sei whale. Their population has been reduced from a total of several million to just a few thousand. Every one of these vanished millions of whales used to consume several hundred tons of a large species of zooplankton a year. That plankton now is undergoing a classic population explosion for want of a predator. What will be the effect on the oxygen producing smaller plankton of the world ocean? What will be the effect on the color and reflectivity of the vast areas of the oceans? What will be the effect on the average water temperature of the oceans, on its dissolved oxygen content and subsequently on the earth's atmosphere? No one knows. But climatologists know any significant change in ocean temperature can have profound effects on the earth's climates. By killing off the whales of the world man is playing Russian roulette with the earth's primary life support system. Yes, we desperately need the whales to preserve the air we breathe. . . .

For thousands of years man has regarded his high relative order of intelligence as confirmation of the belief that all other animals are subordinate to him. In the last few years enough evidence has been found to indicate man may not be alone on top of the pyramid of animal intelligence. The reader will guess at once at the identity of those who may rival us—the whales. The majority of scientists who have studied them agree that several species of whales are so intelligent that no other animal but man can rival them. Much more evidence will be needed before we can accurately measure or compare their intelligence. For the moment at least we are faced with the possibility, I repeat, the possibility, that some species of whales may even surpass man in intelligence. If that should be the case, and if we continue to make progress in our ability to communicate with whales,

Above: *A Japanese watercolor of a right whale and her calf. Unlike early European whalers, who took a disproportionate number of mothers and calves, seventeenth-century Japanese whalers did not hunt females with young. Unfortunately, this foresight was to be the exception rather than the rule in the history of world whaling. (Courtesy of the Kendall Whaling Museum, Sharon, Massachusetts, USA)*

Opposite page: *Charles M. Scammon was an enthusiastic whaler whose depredations on gray whales along the coast of Mexico and California nearly brought about the demise of the species. The frontispiece to his classic work,* The Marine Mammals of North America, *shows ships anchored outside one of the breeding lagoons that he discovered dispatching the whaleboats to kill mother gray whales and their calves. In 1970, Scammon's Lagoon became the first world sanctuary in the world. Today it attracts tourists in whale-watching boats instead of whalers armed with exploding harpoons.*

what may man learn about life, the earth, the oceans?

That's the most important reason why man needs the whales—that, and the fact that all living creatures are related and all are dependent on each other. They are a guide to the spiritual and intellectual route man must follow if he wishes to preserve the beauty and well being of the planet that is home to all living things. Should we fail to learn that lesson, we shall perish with them.

The 1970s saw many changes in the world's attitudes towards whales. In 1972, Mexico declared Scammon's Lagoon the world's first whale sanctuary. The passage of the Marine Mammal Protection Act in the United States that same year made it illegal to import whale products into the United States. In 1975, the environmental activist group Greenpeace began its anti-whaling campaign, exploding into the public consciousness by challenging huge Soviet factory ships on the high seas from small inflatable craft. Canada, the United States, and South Africa all shut down their coastal whaling operations, and the International Whaling Commission declared the Indian Ocean to be a sanctuary for whales. In 1978, Australia became the first country in the world to condemn whaling on moral grounds.

For other countries, however, the decision to continue or cease whaling was one of economics. The Soviets had a huge investment in whaling, having built two enormous factory ships in 1959 and 1961. Cetologist Roger Payne reported sitting through many meetings of the International Whaling Commission listening "to the delegation from the Soviet Union use every trick, every scam, every absurd argument possible to keep their whaling industry alive long enough so that the cost of these two fuel-guzzling white elephants could be amortized." Many feel the Soviet Union discontinued whaling in the latter part of

FRONTISPIECE

WHALING SCENE IN THE CALIFORNIA LAGOONS.

the 1980s in part because their ships were aging and it would have been exorbitantly expensive to refit them.

Commentator David Day explained why the Japanese could not afford to stop whaling. "The answer," he argued, "is that in a cold-blooded mathematical calculation, the yearly loss of the industry is less than the cost of closing down the industry—and the yearly loss may be covered by government subsidy and loans."

In a 1986 BBC documentary, commentator Jeremy Cherfas reported:

> The whaling will stop, but only when it's no longer profitable to whale. The economics of whaling are not very hard to understand: essentially the businessmen who control whaling have two options, they can go after as many whales as possible until there aren't enough left to support the industry, in effect they would be mining a profitable vein; or, they can take just the surplus production for a sustainable yield, milking rather than mining the whales. It seems obvious that milking would make more sense than mining, but sometimes the obvious is wrong. The trouble is that whale numbers increase very slowly indeed—perhaps less than two per cent a year, so that if you go for a sustainable yield all the money you have got tied up in ships and crew will earn a very small return. As a businessman it makes most sense to take all the whales you can, and when all the whales are gone, you simply shift your profits into some other venture. It'll always pay to go after just one more whale. That is why whalers ignore calls to reduce the catch, that is why they break the rules whenever they feel like it. Sustainable whaling will never happen simply because money in the bank grows quicker than whales in the water.

In 1982, faced with the reality of drastically declining whale stocks around the world and correspondingly dismal economic returns, the International Whaling Commission agreed to zero quotas, which went into effect in 1986. For the time being at least, commercial whaling had been shut down. As a result of the global moratorium on commercial whaling, operations such as this sperm whale flensing station in the Azores—described by author Bernard Venables in the 1960s—fell silent:

> Across the smooth blue arc of the bay the whale factory glowed white against the olive fall of Monte da Guia, almost a shimmer in the thin sea light. . . .
>
> The flensing platform lay outside, built into the high flank of Monte da Guia, walled in; on the other side a wall dropped to the beach and the quiet water of the bay. Against the building, facing the flensing platform's slope, there were the ponderous steam winches with massive chains and hooks. The platform's surface was smooth, guttered to drain blood away to settling tanks; the slip fell away, cobbled, steeply down and under the arch by the water. . . .

The flukes of a humpback whale. Today scientists account for individual whales as they monitor population levels around the world. (Photograph © Tom Walker)

A trio of sperm whales swim unmolested, the days of Moby-Dick *long gone. (Photograph © Mark Carwardine/Innerspace Visions)*

. . . The whale was brought up to the slip, and as it stranded there, as the water became opaque with the thick red ooze of its blood, men and boys, barelegged, waded around it, clustering like flies about its head. They had scrapers, sharpened and bent from slips of old iron, fastened to handles; they were scraping the head for blackskin, scraping off the oddly thin, almost membranous skin for use as fishing bait.

Now men, barefooted, in shorts or with pantaloons rolled thigh-high, were laboring down the slipway, dragging the ponderous tackles from the winches. A heavy chain was fastened around the tail, in front of the flukes, and to that the tackles were secured. As the whale began to move slowly up the slip, as the winches steamed and labored, the boys and men came too, still scraping blackskin. The whale went slowly, with a soft, shuffling, rustling sound on the cobbles of the slip, until it was at the top and on the easy slope of the flensing platform; it had not fully stopped when two men were at its head with cutting spades. They were working at once, with spare short economical movements, working with brief downward chops. The sound of it was soft, a chunky softness, like chopping into a soft apple; cutting either side, starting high up, they were making a circlet around the body.

As they went, the cut, almost surgically neat, opened a gape in the dark dull sheen of the blackskin, showing within the blubber, white with a faint rosy tint from the stain of blood. Thus far it did not seem bloody; the blubber looked like a confection, soft but firm, opening firmly to the cut, like white fondant or marshmallow. There was nearly a foot's thickness of the blubber, clean and white and sugary; but then they were through that, through to the tissues beneath, and suddenly the blood was gouting.

The blood flooded from the vast carcass as this grotesque butchery proceeded, running audibly, lapping the legs and feet of the men and flowing in the drainage gutters. Now a wire cable had been put to the head and from there to a smaller winch in the corner of the flensing platform; as the men continued chopping in, slowly the winch dragged, bending the head away from the trunk. With heavier cutting spades the spine was severed, and then, the main artery. The men were standing within the carcass, between head and trunk, chopping, chopping, and the torrent of blood from the big artery burst out, swirled through their legs till they were red to the thighs, ran in torrents through the gutters and down the slip, jumping from stone to stone. In the still water of the bay below the opaque red stain spread slowly. . . .

The smell, that whale-factory smell, lay viscously on the air now; the factory was busy, the tall chimney smoking, the cookers stoked with faya wood, cookers for blubber and cookers for bone. The blubber would be rendered down to oil, the cooked bones dried and ground for bonemeal. The meat was being cut, first into lumps, then, at a trestle, into small cubes that would be dried, not cooked, and made into meal. The whaleboat men had finished their work on the head now; the skull was sawed up, the blubber flensed, the spermaceti taken. In earlier days the spermaceti had been jealously separated, saved apart for its finer quality, but not now; all—blubber-oil and spermaceti—is saved together. The lower jawbones had been put aside; from them, later, there would come the taking of the teeth, "stripping ivory," saving the teeth for scrimshaw.

These abandoned boilers in the Azores are silent testaments to the abrupt cessation of an industry in response to a global outcry against the destruction of whales. (Photograph © Francois Gohier)

I left the factory now, out past the towering cookers, out of the door; suddenly there was other air, no blood, no vast outrageous cuts. There was the clean calm sea beyond the isthmus, the turn of little road winding the flank of Monte da Guia. I turned into it, away from the factory, climbing away above the sea. Suddenly it was quiet and lonely and the air sweet with space.

With commercial whaling for all intents and purposes shut down, people began to take another look at the whales that still swam in the oceans of the world.

These colorful boats at dock on Picos Island in the Azores were last used for whaling in 1986, when Portugal became a member of the European Community. Member countries of the European Union, as it is now called, were part of the international moratorium on whaling that came into effect that same year. (Photograph © Francois Gohier)

Part Four

CELEBRATING WHALES

In the water, whales have become the dominant species,
Without killing their own kind.
In the water, whales have become the dominant species,
Though they allow the resources they use to renew themselves.
In the water, whales have become the dominant species,
Though they use language to communicate, rather than to
eliminate rivals.
In the water, whales have become the dominant species,
Though they do not broodily guard their patch with
bristling security.
In the water, whales have become the dominant species,
Without trading innocence for the pretension of possessions.
In the water, whales have become the dominant species,
Though they acknowledge minds other than their own.
In the water, whales have become the dominant species,
Without allowing their population to reach plague proportions.
In the water, the whale is the dominant species;
An extra-terrestrial, who has already landed . . .
A marine intelligentsia, with a knowledge of the deep.
From space, the planet is blue.
From space, the planet is the territory
Not of humans, but of the whale.

—Heathcote Williams, *Whale Nation*

Left: *From Argentina to Australia, whale-watching is becoming an increasingly popular tourist activity. (Photograph © John Hyde, Wild Things Photography)*
Inset: *In 1972, Mexico declared Scammon's Lagoon to be the first whale sanctuary in the world. Today Mexicans celebrate their gray whales with festivals and fireworks. (Photograph © Marilyn Kazmers / SharkSong)*

TAKING TIME TO LOOK AGAIN

Aboriginal subsistence hunters saw the whale as an integrated part of their circle of life. They needed to hunt whales to survive and the number of whales they took likely posed little threat to whale populations. Commercial hunters of the twelfth century and beyond saw whales as a resource to be harvested and assumed that stocks would last forever. Qualms about whaling, if they ever surfaced, were quickly quashed. This extract from Frank T. Bullen's *The Cruise of the "Cachalot": Round the World After Sperm Whales* published in 1911, describes a whaleman's encounter with a female humpback and her calf in the closing decades of the nineteenth century:

Before it was fairly light we lowered, and paddled as swiftly as possible to the bay where we had last seen the spout overnight. When near the spot we rested on our paddles a while, all hands looking out with intense eagerness for the first sign of the whale's appearance. There was a strange feeling among us of unlawfulness and stealth, as of ambushed pirates waiting to attack some unwary merchantman, or highwaymen waylaying a fat alderman on a country road. We spoke in whispers, for the morning was so still that a voice raised but ordinarily would have reverberated among the rocks which almost overhung us, multiplied indefinitely. A turtle rose ghost-like to the surface at my side, lifting his queer head, and, surveying us with stony gaze, vanished as silently as he came.

What a sigh! One looked at the other inquiringly, but the repetition of that long expiration satisfied us all that it was the placid breathing of the whale we sought somewhere close at hand. The light grew rapidly better, and we strained our eyes in every direction to discover the whereabouts of our friend, but for some minutes without result. There was a ripple just audible, and away glided the mate's boat right for the near shore. Following him with our eyes, we almost immediately beheld a pale, shadowy column of white, shimmering against the dark mass of the cliff not a quarter of a mile away. Dipping our paddles with the utmost care, we made after the chief, almost holding our breath. The harpooner rose, darted once, twice, then gave a yell of triumph that ran re-echoing all around in a thousand eerie vibrations, startling the drowsy peca [fruit bats] in myriads from where they hung in inverted clusters on the trees above. But, for all the notice taken by the whale, she might never have been touched. Close nestled to her side was a youngling of not more, certainly, than five days old, which sent up its baby-spout every now and then about two feet into the air. One long, wing-like fin embraced its small body, holding it close to the massive breast of the tender mother, whose only care seemed to be to protect her young, utterly regardless of her own pain and danger. If sentiment

A southern right whale waves a flipper at the setting sun. (Photograph © Jeff Foott)

A cameraman and a southern right whale contemplate each other in the waters off the coast of Patagonia. Whales, despite their enormous bulk, are generally gentle when they meet people in the water and go out of their way to avoid bumping them with their fins or tail flukes. (Photograph © Bob Cranston/Innerspace Visions)

were ever permitted to interfere with such operations as ours, it might well have done so now; for while the calf continually sought to escape from the enfolding fin, making all sorts of puny struggles in the attempt, the mother scarcely moved from her position, although streaming with blood from a score of wounds. Once, indeed, as a deep-searching thrust entered her very vitals, she raised her massy flukes high in the air with an apparently involuntary movement of agony; but even in that dire time she remembered the possible danger to her young one, and laid the tremendous weapon as softly down upon the water as if it were a feather fan.

So in the most perfect quiet, with scarcely a writhe, nor any sign of flurry, she died, holding the calf to her side until her last vital spark had fled, and left it to a swift despatch with a single lance-thrust. No slaughter of a lamb ever looked more like murder. Nor, when the vast bulk and strength of the animal was considered, could a mightier example have been given of the force and quality of maternal love.

The protest movements of the 1970s drew attention to the mindless destruction of the whale and encouraged worldwide studies of these creatures not as resources to be exploited but as wonders that enrich life on the planet. Today we are beginning to know whales as intelligent individuals with whom we may one day interact. Chance encounters out on the high seas no longer send sailors reaching for their harpoons—or for their prayerbooks. In 1978, Norwegian ethnologist and explorer Thor Heyerdahl was on a five-month voyage from the Persian Gulf to the Red Sea to test the seaworthiness of the *Tigris*, a boat modeled on an ancient Sumerian design. In "The Friendly Whale," published in 1983, he describes what it was like to wake suddenly one night in the Indian Ocean and find himself separated from an enormous whale by nothing more than a few bundles of reeds:

It is a unique experience to be awakened by the sound of someone blowing his nose so loudly that it arouses even an experienced raft voyager accustomed to the most exclusive snoring by men packed together in a tiny bamboo cabin. It gives a thrill of happiness to sit up in the sleeping-bag and stare at the black water beside the open bamboo wall where something solid has emerged, something big and smooth as a water-washed reef and blacker than the dark night outside. If the moon is shining the apparition glistens like a polished shoe, but in all the smoothness is a big, panting blow-hole that leaves no doubt that we have a living whale at our bedside. No matter how often you might have seen a small porpoise tumbling about in some marineland, it is quite different to wake up in intimate contact with a big whale within its own free environment. With a bump of the nose it could break your steering-oars, with a blow from the tail it could smash a fragile vessel to bits. But nothing of the sort happens, as long as you do not run a harpoon into the amiable visitor. The whale, if any surviving animal giant has, has little reason to deal lightly with the tiny human species, yet with all its tremendous body-strength it never touched our vessel nor even scratched loose a reed from the bundles. It made sure never to bump into us even in the pitch dark. At an arm's length it could suddenly come up, with the colossal head pointing straight for us, then it would bow head under and slide like a shadow right beneath our bundles to come up on our other side and resume the journey it had interrupted merely to pass by and say a friendly hello.

What were once seen as monsters are now seen as gentle giants, sensitive to the world around them. In researcher Wade Doak's 1989 book *Encounters with Whales and Dolphins*, Argentine diver Dr. Ricardo Mandojana describes touching a South American right whale in the coastal waters of Peninsula Valdes in Patagonia: "I stroked her side and back gently with my bare hands. The skin felt smooth like slippery rubber. I was surprised to feel a distinct quiver, like the tremors a hand elicits from the skin of a horse when patted near the muzzle. I realized how extremely sensitive the cutaneous surface of this gigantic creature was."

As recently as the 1970s, the U.S. Navy published a pamphlet warning that orcas "attack human beings at every opportunity." Gradually people's fear of orcas is diminishing as we learn that, while some orcas may prey upon other whales, none are known to prey upon human beings. Doak records this encounter between diver Gary Longley and an orca in Tauranga, New Zealand, in August 1986: "Suddenly, out of the blue, one glided below me, tilted a little and stared up. It circled twice, moving closer to hang suspended a metre away, looking at me. Then sinking slightly, it opened its huge jaws and took the end of my flipper in its mouth. I recalled the newsletter accounts [five accounts of orcas approaching people and not harming them] and my fears were relieved. Twice it gently mouthed my fin but with no attempt to bite me. Then the pair swam off."

THE NEED FOR PEACEFUL COEXISTENCE

In our increasingly crowded planet, people are becoming concerned about how to best share the oceans with whales. People actively change the whales' environment, often in ways that are detrimental to the whales. For example, every year, humpback whales become entwined in fishing nets off the coast of Newfoundland, Canada. These entanglements cost fishermen thousands of dollars in lost and broken fishing gear, and they may cost the whales their lives.

Jon Lien, a professor at Memorial University in St. John's, is working to save both the fishermen's livelihoods and the whales. Fred Strebeigh wrote an article about Lien for the June 1992 issue of the *Smithsonian*. Strebeigh recounts that since records began to be kept at the end of the

1970s, increasing numbers of humpbacks have been getting entangled in the nets of inshore family fishermen. Most of the trapped whales are young males, whom Lien likens to "teenage drivers"—inexperienced and somewhat reckless. Once the whales have been caught, however, they learn to steer clear of the nets. The year Strebeigh arrived, Lien was predicting a "great" whale season; to Lien that meant almost no whales at all:

By midsummer along the Newfoundland shore, at the easternmost reach of North America, it's whale season. Wherever you fish, in Bay Bulls or Chance Cove or Joe Batt's Arm, you catch whales. Whatever you're after, cod or salmon or capelin, you catch whales. That's life: You want fish? You get whale.

The Folletts got their whale a year ago. It snagged in the big net that Fred and Ambrosene Follett anchor by the shore to catch codfish, not far from their house in the fishing town of Grand Bank. . . . They knew that the whale, left alone, would probably die, thrash their net to shreds, or both. So they did what you do when you catch a whale: you call the Memorial University of Newfoundland and ask for Prof. Jon Lien.

Five hours later, Jon Lien and his assistant Wayne Barney and I are bobbing in a rubber inflatable, two feet above the head of a midsize humpback. In length it overwhelms us: lay the three of us head to foot, then add our boat, and the whale's 35 feet outstretches us all. In weight, three men and a

Orcas, considered a nuisance and expendable, were once used by the U.S. Navy for target practice. Today reserves are set aside for their protection. At this stretch of shoreline at Robson Bight on Vancouver Island, visitors are warned to stay well away from the animals, who swim into shallow water to play, relax, and rub themselves on the smooth stones of the rocky beach. (Photograph © Jeff Foott)

A humpback whale entangled in a fishing net off the coast of Newfoundland. The seas are getting increasingly crowded and ways have to be found for humans and wildlife to share the oceans. Concerned scientists are developing noisemakers to warn whales away from nets and shipping traffic, and sonar-scanning devices to alert ships to the presence of whales. (Photograph © B & C Alexander/ Innerspace Visions)

boat, we could counterbalance perhaps one-fortieth of this whale; we hover over it like flies.

From above, the humpback's white flanks, seen through the clear Newfoundland water, look like the walls of an aquamarine swimming pool. Its black back looks like oil-slicked tarmac. Its humped black dorsal fin, the fin that gives the humpback its name, has been scraped in the Folletts' net to the color of cut salmon.

To my right, Wayne Barney, a full-time fisherman until he reached age 20 and now a student at Memorial, is holding the whale team's basic tools: a razor-edged knife and a sawed-off hockey stick with a hook where its blade used to be. Directly in front of me, cantilevering outward over the gunwales, wearing diving goggles and snorkel, is Jon Lien. I am holding his ankles.

Jon is face-to-face, underwater, with the whale. It looks tense, wild-eyed. Jon looks for an easy solution: the right place to cut net, if necessary, or the right route to urge the whale toward freedom. With a calmer humpback, Jon might touch it, shove at it, use the boat's rubber gunwale to poke it along—the way a cattleman might prod a cow through a gate. But this whale, eyeing Jon's begoggled face, seems to send a message: "Do not touch." Seeing these wild eyes, Jon keeps our distance—about 12 inches.

Jon emerges from the water smiling (in his goggles looking a bit like a nearsighted walrus) and gives his diagnosis: netting has caught on whale chin, whale beard and whale barnacles—chronic hitchhikers on humpbacks and a major reason why humpbacks snag on nets. He asks Wayne for the hockey stick.

As Jon redescends, his ankles rise. I pin them again. Jon works hard and breathes hard. When he needs air, he first clears his snorkel's blowpipe. Spray drifts over us. When the whale needs air, it clears its own blowpipe—sometimes whinnying like a horse, sometimes snorting like a bull. Spray pours onto us.

As Jon tugs at the netting on the whale's chin, the work finds its rhythm. Jon blows; whale blows; Jon blows; whale blows. This could go on for hours.

I hang onto Jon's ankles and on his every word—yelled at Wayne and me through his snorkel. When the snorkel blurts "Ol' on," I hold harder onto Jon's ankles. When it blurts "Uck"—and at the same moment I see the whale cock its tail, giving us what amounts to a fly's-eye view of a flyswatter—I duck, getting my head below the gunwales. (Earlier, Jon assured me that only one time in ten will a whale actually 'strike'—but then its tail comes as fast as a horse's kick.) When the snorkel blurts, "Eez, 'e's comin'," I'm stumped.

I yell at Wayne, "What's he say?"

"He says," Wayne explains, deadpan, "he sees his cousin."

Naturally Wayne is calmer than I. This is my first trapped whale; Wayne's been aboard for two others. Fortunately for all of us, the man whose ankles I've been clinging to has saved more whales than anyone else in the world—hundreds of them. . . .

As it happened the Folletts were lucky with this reckless young whale. In less than an hour, mostly spent staying away from the tail (it never struck), Jon worked the net almost free. Suddenly, with a tug, the whale was loose. It whipped across the bay, gulping air, and then plunged for the depths. The uprush of water from its flukes created a flat "footprint" on the surface, vast as an Amazonian water lily.

"Nothing I could do to hold him," Jon told the Folletts, as if apologizing. Their net damage, he told them, looked slight—maybe a day of patching. Jon offered to start the patching right then; firmly but gratefully they refused. Next, however, he made an offer they did not reject: he would equip the battered net with his new "whale alarms"— noisemakers, designed to warn whales away from nets. . . .

As Jon strung alarms along the Folletts' net, they began to clank—making an industrious clatter, the sound of elves hammering horseshoes. To a whale, he told Fred, "that sounds like a wall of sound." . . .

Just after New Year's [Jon] sent me a note. Humpbacks had hit like never before. Jon estimated the total number of whale collisions with gear at 1,280, with a cost to fishermen of close to a million dollars. All told, 137 humpbacks were reported trapped in gear—up from the previous year's record of 75. Fifteen died, but 122 survived. The year's last humpback banged into a squid trap in Whiteway in late October. It was the biggest whale season ever.

It is often easier for people to identify with individual animals than with a group. Since the 1980s, considerable time and effort have been expended in saving individual animals who have claimed the media spotlight. In his 1987 work *Whales and Man: Adventures with the Giants of the Deep*, Tim Dietz tells about Humphrey, a humpback whale who lost his way and ended up swimming up the Sacramento River in California in October 1985. Peter Chorney, the senior resident agent with the Law Enforcement Division of the National Marine Fisheries Service in Santa Rosa, California, was in charge of rescuing the wayward whale:

After several failed attempts to drive Humphrey downstream, Chorney's regional office suggested that all rescue operations be suspended until . . . an alternative plan might be available. . . .

Humphrey, meanwhile, had made his way even farther

Roger Payne joins other whale enthusiasts in a small rubber boat near Juneau, Alaska, to watch humpback whales. Best known for his work with singing humpbacks and the right whales of Patagonia, Payne has traveled the world in his quest to help save endangered whales. (Photograph © John Hyde, Wild Things Photography)

One of three gray whales trapped in the ice near Barrow, Alaska, in 1988. The world held its breath as the media televised images of the efforts to create a channel so that the whales could escape into open water. Eventually, a Soviet icebreaker came to complete work started by local Inupiat whale hunters and the U.S. military. (Photograph © Francois Gohier)

north, squeezing between the narrow pilings of the Liberty Island Bridge and entering Shag Slough, a 10-foot-deep, dead-end channel less than 30 miles from the state capital, Sacramento. . . . He could go no farther. . . . Humphrey remained extremely active, swimming in circles and occasionally rolling over on his side to slap the water's sur–face with his 15-foot white pectoral fins, delighting the crowds of media people and tourists on the shore, most of whom had never seen a humpback whale, much less one this close. . . .

Dr. Kenneth Norris, a noted marine mammal expert from the University of California at Santa Cruz, suggested trying a Japanese dolphin-driving technique called oikoime to move the whale. The technique involved the use of several water-filled pipes, each about eight feet long and two inches in diameter, which are set over the side of a boat and tapped lightly with hammers to create a pinging sound. . . .

Early on Thursday the rescuers lined up their boats in a neat semicircle upstream of Humphrey, lifted the lengthy pipes over the gunwales, and in unison began banging the pipes with hammers, careful not to make the sound too intense to avoid frightening the animal. Humphrey's response was immediate: He twisted his hulking body and began swimming toward the bridge at the southern end of the slough.

This was on October 24. Humphrey did not leave the Sacramento River until November 4, after twenty-five days in fresh water. Since then, he has been spotted on a number of occasions swimming off the California coast. In October 1990, the hapless Humphrey stranded on a mudbank in San Francisco Bay and had to be freed, once again.

In 1988, musician and whale observer Jim Nollman took part in the rescue of three gray whales trapped in the ice near Barrow, Alaska. The whales had failed to make it to the open sea before the ice closed in around them. Nollman records his encounter will these whales in his 1999 book *The Charged Border: Where Whales and Humans Meet*:

A helicopter lifts me, along with six other journalists, out to the site of the gray whale rescue. It lands, disgorges its passengers, and lifts off to pick up another load of reporters and saviors waiting in Barrow a few miles away. The hush of the winter Arctic rushes in from all sides. There is no wind this morning. I pick up my bag full of underwater acoustic gear, a tape recorder, and a half-size guitar, and saunter over to the scene of the action.

Three whales bob up and down in a round black hole rimmed in white. They lie on the surface for a full two minutes, breathing easily with cavernous two-second-long exhalations. A prolonged three-second breath signifies a change. Together, the whales dunk beneath the surface, disappearing completely out of sight and sound, and for such a long period of time that we might easily forget what on earth has impelled us onto this formless Arctic ice sheet in the first place. My eyes wander over the theater of the rescue operation. To the south, two great chopping helicopters unload journalists and cameramen directly onto the ice. To the east, a three-foot-high escarpment of solid ice runs along the shoreline all the way out to the horizon, looking as if the last wave of a long-forgotten summer had frozen as it curled in upon itself. To the north, a white plain of sea ice charges unbroken. I blink, unable to locate even the hint of a landmark.

The local Inupiat help the U.S. military carve out a channel in the ice leading to open water. Nollman's plan is to encourage the whales to swim along the channel by playing music to them:

> I step inside the shed, followed by two of the Inupiats. I hand each man a pair of headphones and explain that everything they are about to hear is produced underwater. They listen a moment; hear nothing, but then register a slursh as one of the whales creates turbulence against the hydrophone. I twist the volume control of the tape recorder . . . , sigh deeply, and push the play button. I notice the faces of my two companions brighten, a sign that the harmonies of Ladysmith Black Mombazo have begun to course through the dark water.
>
> The whales dive out of sight.
>
> I step outside the shed. Stand alongside eight or nine Inupiat watching the empty, smooth water. A minute passes. The crowd grows to fifteen people. Two minutes pass. Several people shout at once, "Look, there they are! . . . Too mu-u-uch!" The three whales have resurfaced at the other hole. . . . I rush into the shed and turn off the tape. The whales immediately dive again. A minute passes. We are all scanning the water for some sign of them. Suddenly they surface right in front of us. "Oh no!" someone shouts. "Turn the music back on!" Everyone starts yelling at me to play it again. Not thinking anymore, I press the play button.
>
> The three whales dive together. No one speaks. Everyone darts their eyes back and forth between the two holes. Two minutes pass. Three minutes. Where have they gone? Finally a keen-eyed rescuer shouts, "Look! There they are. Way down there." He points his finger a good quarter mile down the length of the channel. Yes, I see them as well. We all see them; one whale blows, then another one. The whales have found the channel! Success! Everyone is smiling broadly; a few people are jumping up and down. I am patted on the back several times.

Humpbacks regularly breach, propelling themselves vertically out of the water before coming down on their sides with a resounding crash. They may repeat this activity up to twenty times in a row. When they are not breaching, they may slap the water with their pectoral fins or tail flukes, making a great deal of noise, perhaps to communicate with other whales in the area. (Photograph © Francois Gohier)

After the whales set off down the channel, one drowned, likely a victim of exhaustion. A few days later, a Soviet icebreaker arrived on the scene and led the two remaining whales to the safety of the open seas. The U.S. and Soviet military, a group of Inupiat whale hunters, and one underwater music maker had combined forces under the watchful eye of world media to save two representatives of a species that one hundred years before had been hunted with such relish.

MAKING CONTACT?

As we spend more time observing whales rather than killing them, we are learning that cetaceans seem to have a capacity for direct interaction with us, sometimes it even seems they have a sense of humor. Among the most playful of whales are humpbacks, which are found off the coasts of Alaska, Hawaii, and the northeastern United States. In *Whales and Man*, Tim Dietz recounts the antics of a humpback known as Colt in June 1984 off the coast of Massachusetts:

> Friendly dolphins have been known for centuries, but only in the past few years has the phenomenon of friendly great whales emerged. Granted, it isn't easy to imagine a 45-foot, 40-ton, knob-faced, barnacle-encrusted giant as cute or huggable, but some certainly seem that way. Believe me, I met one.
>
> In June 1984, I was . . . cohosting a whale watch with naturalist Scott Mercer aboard the Cetacea out of Newburyport, Massachusetts. The weather that morning wasn't promising. Thick fog enveloped the dock and the crowd of people anxiously waiting to board the vessel. Because the forecast called for continued fog throughout the day, Mercer offered his passengers a choice to go another day or proceed with the trip in the hope we would spot some whales in the limited visibility. They chose to go, and as it turned out, no one regretted it.
>
> Three hours after we entered the Gulf of Maine, the 80 or so people aboard were getting quite anxious. Visibility had remained poor, and Mercer and I, along with Captain Billy Neelon, were peering into the gray mist to catch sight of a cetacean or two. We were clipping along at a brisk 17 knots when suddenly, like a gigantic cork, a large humpback burst to the surface a mere 40 yards off our bow. Neelon, no doubt with his heart in his throat, threw the engines into reverse and eased the vessel into a slow drift.
>
> Fortune was with us, for this was no ordinary whale. It was Colt, probably one of the most playful humpbacks in the North Atlantic. Within moments he began his antics: lying on his back and slapping his mighty pectoral fins on the surface; rubbing his belly and grooved throat on the hull; spyhopping to take a good look at us; and then what I call "spraying"— his peculiar habit of blowing into the faces of unsuspecting

MIND IN THE WATERS

The whale rolls unseen through the water, steady, sure, alert. On the surface a small group of people drift in a rubber boat, wait for the appearance of the whale. The whale rolls like a great wheel, turning over smoothly, silently. It is night. There is nothing to see except the calm dark surface of the sea. Then the water parts, reveals the rolling back. The blowhole of the whale opens and the sound of her breathing deepens the silence. She continues her long, steady motion, rolling back into the sea from where she came. . . .

As I recollect the whales, I realize how strange they are to me—these enormous, cumbersome, yet supremely graceful beings that move like monsters out of the past, beneath the surface of the sea. I envy them, envy their life and the ease of their connections. I wish to be of them, yet my thoughts, my ideas, become obstacles to the possibility of the experience.

This is the mind I have always believed existed somewhere. The deep calm mind of the ocean, connected to body, living *in* the world, not looking out at it. Surrounded by the gentle clicking of each other's sound, these creatures drift and dive, carve shining bubbled circles in the still water, move like dream ghosts out of the sea's unchanging past.

—Joan McIntyre, *Mind in the Waters* (1974)

spectators leaning over the rail for a better look.

Colt is one of more than 250 humpbacks given nicknames by Gulf of Maine scientists who photo-identify humpbacks by distinctive pigmentation patterns on the undersides of their flukes. Colt was first spotted off the Massachusetts coast as a yearling calf in 1981 and was so named because of his unusually feisty and curious behavior, even for a calf. Three years later, he hadn't mellowed a bit.

Colt continued his salty show for well over an hour, at times approaching the dazzled spectators within touching distance before disappearing beneath the boat. I stood on the bridge, camera in hand, enjoying the clarity of the water, which was accentuated by the grayish light conditions of the day. Then I saw it—his eye—several feet below the surface, staring hard at me. He had no doubt decided to take a moment or two just to watch the watchers, curious about the tiny visitors suspended above his watery world. Within moments he was gone.

Since Dietz wrote this piece, the catalog of humpbacks in the Gulf of Maine has expanded and now stands at more than 1,100 animals. This is the best-known population of whales in the world, with sighting histories of three generations of identified individuals going back to 1975.

The desire to observe whales more closely has led to dramatic changes in the way we think about them. For instance, the gray whales of Mexico—those "devilfish" who had a reputation for viciously

attacking whalers—are now known as "the friendly whales." In 1977, Bill and Mia Rossiter were among members of a three-boat expedition to San Ignacio Lagoon, a breeding lagoon for the Pacific gray whale. While they were there, a most extraordinary event happened: a female began to lift their boat on her head:

> She was very gentle with us. Then she moved about softly, tucking her flippers in close, rubbing and pushing us, and turning repeatedly. Her enormous tail never came near. She was positively cautious. We could easily have been overturned. Even her breathing was restrained near us.
>
> Vertical alongside, her rostrum just above the surface, we began to touch her. We crooned "Amazing Grace" as we rubbed the smooth skin and felt a gentle return. A flipper was presented, motionless and dripping, inches away. We pulled it. The whale seemed to come closer, as if we had really moved her. Then the incredible mouth opened and we rubbed gums and baleen—yellowish, dripping and wonderfully close. "Amazing Grace," as my wife decided to call her, presented the entire forward third of her body to us, purposefully.
>
> With mask and underwater camera, I hung over the side and peered into the sun-rayed green-brown haze of the lagoon. Below us she rose like a grey cloud. Then she rolled upside down beneath the boat, her pectoral fins straddling us. With absolute grace and control, she lifted us on her chest between her massive flippers. Then she came up again from behind me, her rostrum gliding within reach. Gently she rolled on her side and paused. We were looking at each other.
>
> Another time, I placed my hand on her rostrum and pushed—and was pushed back. Again and again she returned at all possible angles and attitudes. Once she paused as her blowhole came by and released a frothy mass of bubbles that boiled around the boat. We had seen whales do this with each other. It certainly seemed to say something. This whale did everything possible to relate, probably testing us in more ways than we knew. Was she toying with us or was she just curious? It all seemed beyond mere play; her concern and caution, her bubbles and noises.

This anecdote related by cetologist Roger Payne suggests such behavior may extend beyond the confines of the breeding lagoon:

> Biologist Jim Darling told me about a gray whale that a policeman on Vancouver Island reported to him because it had "rammed" the policeman's boat. The waters off Vancouver Island are a major Canadian tourist area as well as a summer feeding ground for a few gray whales. The policeman was concerned as to whether he ought not do something about the whale, since it might represent a threat to boaters in the

A gray whale calf in Magdalena Bay, Mexico. Philippe Cousteau, son of the famous French diver Jacques Cousteau, describes his first underwater encounter with a gray whale: "I could see, somewhat fuzzily, its immense mouth—a mouth unlike any I had ever seen before. And then I saw its body as it swam past me. Its movements seemed incomparably supple; they were not separate motions, but one beautifully co-ordinated action. I was struck by the hydrodynamic perfection of its power, by its invincibility." (Photograph © Marilyn Kazmers/SharkSong)

A friendly gray whale in Mexico's San Ignacio Lagoon. The descendants of gray whales who were once harpooned in these waters now vie for the tourists' attention, presenting backs and baleen to be rubbed. (Photograph © Tom Walker)

area. As they discussed the incident Jim asked the policeman whether the whale had rolled belly-up after ramming his boat, to which the man replied, "Why yes, as a matter of fact it did." Jim suggested that there was nothing wrong with the whale. It probably just wanted to be patted.

People are increasingly intrigued by the possibility of communicating with whales. This encounter off the coast of British Columbia was recorded by Jim Nollman in 1986, the same man who would be called to the rescue of the gray whales two years later: "The very best night was when we had a Tibetan Lama chanting. Ten orca were within 50 metres of the boat. One came close to the underwater speaker. The whales were silent. When the chanting ceased they began whistling and grunting loudly. Then the lama was joined by violin, guitar and electric organ. The whales vocalised with us, sliding their notes up and down scale to meet ours."

Payne feels there seems to be a bond between people and whales, "as though our two mammalian brains have more in common than we are aware and that we really may have significant things to say to each other—despite our isolation for the last sixty-five million years—if only we could find a communication channel." One of the reasons for this, he says, is because many people react strongly to the sounds whales make; it is as though they strike a chord deep in our mammalian brain. As Payne describes it, "In the darkness of the abyss another manifestation of life permeates everything—the calls of distant whales. They carry over vast distances, the sounds traveling in long, majestically curving paths and completely filling the vast, vaulted spaces—at times echoing off the ceiling a mile or two overhead, or off the oozy floor as far beneath. To many human ears these sounds are very beautiful."

Diver Sylvia Earle describes being underwater when a humpback whale was singing:

> Underwater, the sound of a singing whale at close range is so intense that the air spaces in our head and body seem to vibrate. Once, after locating a singer by listening for the appropriate sequence using underwater microphones lowered from the boat, Chuck, Al and I lowered ourselves over the side and settled to the sea floor, 120 feet below. Chuck's eyes acknowledged the ethereal quality of what was happening. Although we could not see a whale, shafts of light beamed around us while eerie "wheeps" and low rumbling sighs assailed our ears, our whole bodies. We could feel as well as hear the song as it ranged from ultra-low bass through bubbling, rippling sequences, hee-haws, then to high, violin-like squeals. It seems that the whale was equipped simultaneously with an orchestra—and a barnyard.

The oceans are filled with the sounds made by whales. Fin and blue whales make the loudest sounds ever attributed to an animal. Humpback whales sing hauntingly beautiful songs. Beluga whales are known as sea canaries because of the variety of their vocalizations. Orcas off the northwest coast of North America are divided into pods according to the dialects they use to communicate with one another. One extensively studied pod has maintained the same dialect for the past thirty years. Sperm whales use patterns of clicks to communicate.

In the 1960s, biologists tried to translate the whistles and clicks of cetaceans into English or sign language. Dolphins were trained to understand simple commands, but a true understanding of "whale language" proved elusive. We do not even know if whales "hear" sounds as we do. For instance, the echoes heard by toothed whales as they bounce a series of clicks off objects to ascertain their locations and physical properties are likely interpreted as three-dimensional moving images rather than as the one-dimensional sounds that humans hear. We do not know if humans and whales will ever be able to bridge the gulf that divides the different ways that they interpret their worlds. Nor do we know if human beings will ever be able to map the workings of the whale brain.

Occasionally, however, a bridge does seem within our grasp. In "Physty," whale enthusiast and researcher Guy D'Angelo describes a fleeting moment of connection with a young sperm whale who was recuperating in an unused boat basin after having tried to beach himself on the south shore of Long Island in April 1981:

> During the day [Physty] would mostly log around, sleeping or being lazy. In the evenings he would come to life; actively swimming and click-training the pier posts and everything in the basin with his "sonar."
>
> His clicks were just unbelievable. When you were standing on this solid wooden dock, or bulkhead filled with dirt, there was no air space between you and the water. When Physty clicked in your direction, you could actually feel the vibration of his clicks coming up through the soles of your shoes.
>
> One cold evening we were standing on the dock. People were stamping their feet to keep warm, and all of a sudden Physty is answering their stamps. He was mimicking what they were stamping, with his clicks.
>
> My wife picked this up and started playing a little game with him, stamping in sequences. He would mimic stamps up to five beats. In other words you could do 2-3, 4-1, any combination up to five beats and he would repeat it accurately. After five beats he would give you a very BR-BR-BR-BR-BR-BR-BR-BR click-train, as if to say, "I don't want to play this game this way. Give me five beats."
>
> We remembered this for years. I believe the January, 1993 issue of the *Journal for Marine Mammalogy* published data about sperm whale codas. The data had been collected in both the South Pacific and the South Atlantic in 1981....

When male humpback whales sing, they hang motionless with their heads down, filling the surrounding waters with eerie sounds that ebb and flow with the ocean currents. (Photograph © James D. Watt/ Innerspace Visions)

An adult sperm whale spyhopping in the northern Sea of Cortez, Mexico. Henry David Thoreau asked: "Can he who has discovered only some of the values of whale-bone and whale oil be said to have discovered the true use of the whale? Can he who slays the elephant for his ivory be said to have 'seen the elephant'? These are petty and accidental uses; just as if a stronger race were to kill us in order to make buttons and flageolets of our bones." (Photograph © Michael S. Nolan/Innerspace Visions)

Over 50% of the transmissions of these whales were five-beat codas. There were identifying themselves, like tribal identification, with a five-beat coda.

So what Physty must have been doing is trying to find out what our coda was. We were probably confusing him no end, because we changed our beat rhythm all the time. He kept repeating whatever we stamped, but we kept changing what we stamped. He was trying to find out what tribe or pod we belonged to, but he never got the same answer twice. . . .

That evening there was a strong wind blowing, and Physty sailed downwind into the corner of the boat basin where I was standing. I knelt down and I patted him on the top of his head, pretty close to his blowhole, because that was the only part of the whale out of the water.

Physty had obviously put his tail on the bottom; that's the only way he could have done this: he proceeded to slowly, and I mean very slowly, lift his whole head out of the water in front of me.

Within 30 or 40 seconds I was faced with this huge head! Of course, I couldn't see very much because it was quite dark. But I could see the outline of it, towering above me.

Then he started to click-train me. Very rapid BR–BR–BR–BR–BR–BR–BR–BR–BR–BR–BR–BR–BR–BR–BR–BR–BR–BR–BR–BR–BR! Just like that. It was like standing in front of a big woofer speaker. I could feel the higher pitched sounds going up and down my body. I was kneeling so it started at my knees going through my torso, lung area and up to my head.

Meanwhile, I was petting him all around, feeling this huge bulbous nose. I reached around and felt the indentations underneath his upper jaw, the sockets where his teeth would eventually grow. I felt his lower jaw and the little teeth buds on the very tip of the jaw. He just had little budding teeth.

All the while I was talking to him. "Hello, how are you? How ya doing? What 'cha doing, boy?"

I put my hand on the notch where his head curved in a little bit and then curved out again to form the top of the upper jaw. And right in the notch was the focal point of the sound. That's where the "monkey's fist" is located, as the old whalers used to call it: the valve that's underneath the blowhole, where the two airways meet just before going out to the single blowhole. That's where they merge, and that's where the cartilaginous plate is. And, that's where he produces the sound. It was obvious, by putting my hand right there, that was where the sound was most intense.

We stood there together for at least three minutes. Both exploring one another: me with my hand, and my eyes as best I could in the dark; and him, of course, with his sonications.

THE FUTURE

Some people believe that it is only by getting to know whales that we will care enough about them to want to help them survive. Most of us, if we know whales at all, know them from captive orcas and belugas in aquaria. Roger Payne speaks to this experience:

> There is one major way in which aquariums may be benefiting their occupants and, by extension, the rest of life on earth. It is the example . . . [of] a child standing transfixed before an underwater window, watching the grace and beauty of the animals swimming on the other side of the glass. What is she learning at that moment? How long will it affect her behavior toward whales, and by extension toward nature? How much are such moments worth to her? More importantly, how much are they worth to the whales?

Perhaps in this age of travel, however, it is no longer necessary to bring the whales to the people but, rather, bring the people to the whales.

Whalewatching tours are becoming increasingly popular the world over; ecological arguments aside, in the long run, keeping whales alive could be more lucrative than killing them. Certainly, most of us who have viewed whales, whether in captivity or in the wild, feel the experience has added to our lives in some intangible way. Canadian writer Josef Skvorecky's essay "Bubbles the Whale" describes this feeling:

> On the roof of the tower there are several large pools where aquatic creatures, purported to be the most intelligent beings next to man himself, are performing. Dolphins, those strange sages of the Californian seas. What they are doing looks like a kind of co-ordinated gymnastic dance. On a command from the trainer, for instance, a trio of the mammals dive to the bottom of the deep pool, then race to the surface, break through with all their might, and execute— in perfect formation, like circus horses—a slow, magnificent, high leap. Three aerodynamic bodies in line describe exactly the same arc and then, sharp noses foremost, cut back into their natural element like a knife slicing into butter. And again and again, five, ten times in a row. They can also walk on the water, by rearing up on their tails and thrashing them rapidly, an action that propels them backwards to the opposite end of the pool.
>
> But there is another creature in the aquarium who steals the show from the dolphins, as they say in show business. For a gigantic body can be seen moving among the dolphins, who stick their heads out of the water after each performance and await their reward in the form of a fish. This body is four times larger than the biggest dolphin, like a submersible railway car. It too thrusts its huge, spherical head out of the

A killer whale in a Sea World show in Orlando, Florida. Killer whales and beluga whales are the only great whales that are regularly kept in captivity. People today raise ethical questions about confining animals that were never meant to be kept enclosed. (Photograph © Robert E. Barber)

water for a fish. Bubbles the Whale, the program calls it, and says that he is supposed to be a less intelligent but rather more massive brother of the intellectuals of the sea. And when they command the dolphins to dance, Bubbles the Whale eagerly spins on his own axis through the water to the rhythm of a foxtrot, and when they are ordered to walk on the water this enormous cylinder of flesh rises up and, thrashing his tail so energetically that he drenches the little girls standing by the guard rail, he overcomes the forces of gravity and shoots diagonally across the pool like an upright torpedo. It is as if the world's fattest fat lady were dancing the cancan with a line of svelte and sexy chorus girls. And at last, when the trainer is lifted high above the pool on a mechanical crane and, one by one, the dolphins shoot out of the water to a height of perhaps five metres to snatch a fish from his hands and then plummet back into the agitated pool with it, suddenly two policemen appear and begin energetically pushing the crowds away from the side of the pool. Why this sudden display of force? Then I understand. When the team of dolphins has finished taking turns, a rolling of drums comes from the loudspeakers, a clamorous, nerve-racking noise, as when artistes on the flying trapeze prepare to perform the salto mortale; then the water, moved from somewhere in the deep, begins to churn and boil, the surface breaks, and out of it, like a flying tank, rises that corpulent creature of the sea. He attains the same height as the dolphins, opens his huge maw, and gently plucks a two-foot cod straight from the trainer's hand.

At that moment, however, he appears to lose all interest in balance. He twists into a horizontal position and then falls—very slowly, it seems—and crashes in utterly unaerodynamic fashion, with all his many tons, into the water. A several-thousand-gallon tidal wave rises out of the pool on either side, and the astonished boys who have snuck back to the guard-rail behind the policemen's backs flee to their mothers, drenched to the skin. Bubbles the Whale—a creature from a Walt Disney cartoon.

A few days later, on the advice of experts, I stand on the westernmost point of the deserted peninsula of Point Reyes, north of San Francisco, a chimera-like finis terrae of the Californian coast. Bubbles the Whale, that sweet, trained cetacean, that corpulent water-ballet dancer, has filled me with the desire to see his free brothers and sisters. And see them I do: but only as black shadows moving just below the surface of the green water and as slender columns of delicate steam rising from it, testifying to the fact that these ladies and gentlemen are not fish, but members of the marine intelligentsia. They pass by Point Reyes on their millenia-old journey through the Pacific, with their twenty-foot calves.

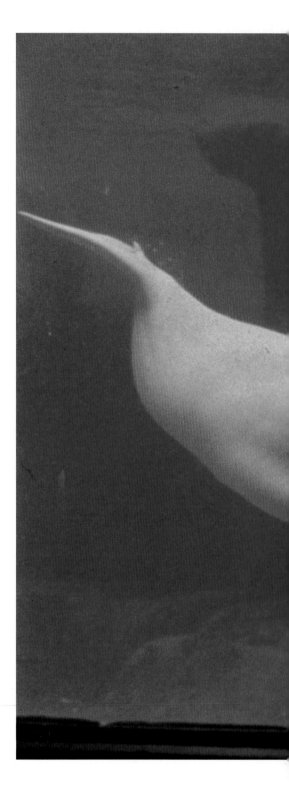

A child gazes at a beluga whale at Vancouver Aquarium. Aquaria are an important way to bring people into close contact with whales and thus further their knowledge about the creatures of the sea. But many argue that it is better to bring humans to the whales. (Photograph © Jeff Vinnick / Vancouver Aquarium Marine Science Centre)

Once again, I feel that I have been touched by the hand of an eternal and impenetrable mystery.

The challenge lies in translating the feelings that whales engender in us into global action to ensure that future generations of whales will swim in the oceans when future generations of humans live on the land. In 1976, Greg Gatenby wrote in his introduction to *Whale Sound*, an anthology of poetry about whales, "God knows we have harmed enough things on this planet, but to remove the largest animals God ever made seems to declare an arrogance and shortsightedness that speaks volumes more about the intelligence of homo sapiens than any great mathematical equation or work of art." Cetologist Roger Payne agrees. He believes that the way we treat whales shows the measure of our souls.

In 1980, Dr. Michael Fox, an author and veterinarian, made the following speech at the Ethics of Whaling Conference:

> The concern for the future of whales is a positive sign of spiritual awakening and the birth of eco-consciousness. Let us not lose our faith, courage and commitment. The ethical, human and ecological crises of today can be seen in a positive light as shaping forces in our own evolution and transformation. We are entering a new age of earth-mind and earth-minding. Our greatest challenge is to begin the awesome task of healing the earth and transforming human consciousness while there is still time. In the restoration of the earth we will realize our true human potentials and rejoice not in our own creations, but with all of creation in empathetic resonance and communion with the whale, the wolf and the eagle of whose essence is the significant "otherness" of our being and becoming.

The reprieve from commercial whaling given to whales since 1986 has improved their condition. The question is whether we can sustain and enhance this improvement by responding appropriately to the whales' situation and whether we can safeguard the health of the planet as a whole—both for our sake and for the sake of the whales.

Blue whale flukes at sunset. Our lives are enriched by the presence of whales. (Photograph © Tom Walker)

SELECTED WHALE STATISTICS

ODOTOCETES (TOOTHED WHALES)

Sperm Whale (Physeter macrocepalus)
Distribution: Worldwide in temperate waters; bulls in polar regions; rarely enter shallow waters. **Size:** Males 59 ft (18 m), 50 to 77 tons (45 to 70 metric tonnes); females 39 ft (12 m) and 16 to 22 tons (15 to 20 metric tonnes). **Age at sexual maturity:** Females 7 to 12 years; males 18 to 19 years. Males not socially mature until they are 26 years old. **Life expectancy:** Up to 75 years. Single calf every five years. **Diet:** Large pelagic squid and other cephalopods, and medium to large fish. **Social units:** Bachelor schools and breeding schools of 20 to 25 animals, although they may gather in the hundreds; old males tend to be solitary.

Killer Whale (Orcinus orca)
Distribution: Worldwide. **Size:** Males up to 21 to 28 ft (6.5 to 8.5 m), 11 tons (10 metric tonnes); females 20 to 21 ft (6 to 6.5 m), 8 tons (7 metric tonnes). **Age at sexual maturity:** 8 to 10 years. **Life expectancy:** 50 to 100 years. Females reproduce at intervals of 2 to 14 years. **Diet:** Residents eat fish; transients also eat birds, sea turtles, and other mammals. **Social units:** Maternal pods of 5 to 25 animals.

Beluga Whale (Delphinapterus leucas)
Distribution: Wide but discontinuous circumpolar in the northern hemisphere; some populations migrate. **Size:** 10 to 16 ft (3 to 5 m), 1,100 to 3,300 lb (500 to 1,500 kg). **Age at sexual maturity:** Females 5 years, males 8 years. **Life expectancy:** 30 to 40 years. **Diet:** Arctic cod, herring, smelt, flounder, sand lance, crustaceans, mollusks, and other benthic invertebrates. **Social units:** Groups of 5 to 20 animals; hundreds around river mouths in the summer.

Narwhal (Monodon monoceros)
Distribution: Discontinuous circumpolar in the northern hemisphere. **Size:** 13 to 16.5 ft (4 to 5 m); 1,760 to 3,520 lb (800 to 1,600 kg). **Age at sexual maturity:** Females 4 to 7 years, males 8 to 9 years. **Life expectancy:** 30 to 40 years. Single calf every 3 years. **Diet:** Squid, bottom fish, and crustaceans. **Social units:** Groups of 20 animals; thousands may travel together.

MYSTICETES (BALEEN WHALES)

In general, all species of baleen whales are found either alone or in unstable groups. The latter are generally small (pairs are common for most species). Larger, non-social groups may form at feeding grounds and aggregations of a social nature occur during the breeding season.

Gray Whale (Eschrichtius robustus)
Distribution: Two main stocks—one from Baja California to Bering and Chukchi Seas; other from South Korea to Okhotsk Sea; in Arctic feeding grounds in winter, migrates to southern breeding grounds in summer. **Size:** 49 ft (15 m), 37 tons (34 metric tonnes). **Age at sexual maturity:** 5 to 11 years. **Life expectancy:** Up to 77 years. Single calf every 2 years. **Diet:** Bottom feeders; eat small fish and a wide variety of invertebrates.

Right Whale (Eubalaena australis, Eubalaena glacialis)
Distribution: Temperate waters of both hemispheres. Southern right whales are circumpolar between 20 and 55 degrees south; migrate south to Antarctica for summer. Small concentrations of Northern Right Whales in North Atlantic and North Pacific. **Size:** 16 to 60 ft (5 to 18 m), 33 to 88 tonnes (30 to 80 metric tonnes). **Age at sexual maturity:** Females 5 to 10 years. **Life expectancy:** 70 years. Single calf every 3 to 4 years. **Diet:** Skim feed on the surface and below water on copepods and krill.

Bowhead Whale (Balaena mysticetus)
Distribution: Close to the Arctic pack; short seasonal migrations. Four distinct populations—Davis Strait, Baffin Bay, northern Hudson Bay, and Foxe Basin; Bering, Chukchi, and Beaufort Seas; Sea of Okhotsk; and North Atlantic. **Size:** 11 to 66 ft (3 to 20 m), 66 to 110 tons (60 to 100 metric tonnes). **Age at sexual maturity:** 15 to 20 years. **Life expectancy:** 100 years. Single calf every 3 to 4 years. **Diet:** Crustaceans and invertebrates.

Humpback Whale (Megaptera novaeangliae)
Distribution: Worldwide; winters in low-latitude breeding grounds and summers in high-latitude feeding grounds; northern and southern hemisphere populations are thought not to mix; population in Indian Ocean may not migrate. **Size:** 62 ft (19 m), 44 to 53 tonnes (40 to 48 metric tonnes). **Age at sexual maturity:** 5 years. **Life expectancy:** 50 years or more. Single calf every 1 to 3 years. **Diet:** Krill and small fish.

Blue Whale (Balaenoptera musculus)
Distribution: Worldwide. **Size:** 98 ft (30 m), 200 tons (181 metric tonnes). **Age at sexual maturity:** 10 years. **Life expectancy:** 80 years. Single calf every 2 to 3 years. **Diet:** Krill.

Fin Whale (Balaenoptera physalus)
Distribution: Worldwide; prefers temperate waters; some populations may migrate. **Size:** 89 ft (27 m), 140 tons (127 metric tonnes). **Age at sexual maturity:** 5 to 6 years. **Life expectancy:** Up to 100 years. Single calf every 2 to 3 years. **Diet:** Krill and small schooling fish.

Sei Whale (Balaenoptera borealis)
Distribution: Worldwide; may migrate to low latitudes in winter. **Size:** 69 ft (21 m), 22 to 33 tons (20 to 30 metric tonnes). **Age at sexual maturity:** 6 to 12 years. **Life expectancy:** Up to 75 years. Single calf every 2 to 3 years. **Diet:** Skim feeds for copepods; also krill, small fish, and squid.

WORKS CITED AND ADDITIONAL RESOURCES

Acorn, Milton. "Whale Poem." In Gatenby, *Whale Sound*, 13.

Anon. *The Book of The Thousand and One Nights*: Rendered into English from the Literal and Complete French Translation of Dr. J. C. Mardrus by Powys Mathers, vol. 2. London: Bibliophile Books, 1964.

Aristotle. *Historia Animalium*. Translated by D'Arcy Wentworth Thompson. Oxford: Clarendon Press, 1910.

Arrian. *History of Alexander and Indica*. Loeb Classical Library. Cambridge, Mass.: Harvard University Press, 1983.

Attungana, Patrick. "Address to the Alaskan Eskimo Whaling Commission." Reprinted in the *Open Lead* (1) 2:16ff. Translated by James Nageak.

Atwood, Margaret. "The Afterlife of Ishmael." In Gatenby, *Whales: A Celebration*, 210.

Boas, Franz. *The Central Eskimo, 6th Annual Report, Bureau of American Ethnology, 1884–85*. Washington D.C.: Government Printing Office, 1888.

——————. *Kwakiutl Tales*, vol. 2. New York: Columbia University Press, 1910.

——————. *The Religion of the Kwakiutl Indians*. New York: Columbia University Press, 1930.

——————. *Tsimshian Texts, American Ethnological Society, vol. III*. Leyden: E. J. Brill, 1912.

Bullen, Frank T. *The Cruise of the "Cachalot": Round the World After Sperm Whales*. London: Smith, Elder, 1911.

Caduto, Michael J. and Joseph Bruchac. *Keepers of the Animals: Native American Stories and Wildlife Activities for Children*. Golden, Colo.: Fulcrum, 1991.

Chambers Books of Days: A Miscellany of Popular Antiquities. London: W.R. Chambers, 1863.

Cherfas, Jeremy. "Battle for the Whales." Television documentary. London: BBC, aired June 1986.

Clarke, Robert D. *Sperm Whales of the Azores. Discovery Reports*. Cambridge: Institute of Oceanographic Sciences, University of Cambridge, 1954.

Cousteau, Jacques-Yves and Philippe Diolé, *The Whale*. Translated from the French by J. F. Bernard. Arrowood Press: New York, 1987.

Curtis, Edward S. *Indian Days of the Long Ago*. New York: World Book Company, 1915.

——————. *The North American Indian (Nootka),* vol. 11. New York: World Book Company, 1916.

D'Angelo, Guy. "Physty." In *Whale Tales: Human Interactions with Whales*, vol. 1. Peter J. Fromm, collector. Friday Harbor, WA: Whale Tales Press, 1996.

Darling, James D., Charles "Flip" Nicklin, Kenneth S. Norris, Hal Whitehead, and Bernd Wörsig. *Whales, Dolphins and Porpoises*. Washington, D.C.: National Geographic Society, 1995.

Day, David. *The Whale War*. San Francisco: Sierra Club Books, 1987.

Dietz, Tim. *Whales and Man: Adventures with the Giants of the Deep*. Dublin, N.H.: Yankee Books, 1987.

Dixon, Roland B. *The Mythology of All Races*, vol. 9, Oceanic. Boston: Marshall Jones, 1816.

Doak, Wade. "Encounters with Grey Whales in Mexico." In *Encounters with Whales and Dolphins*. London: Hodder and Stoughton, 1989.

D'Vincent, Cynthia. *Voyaging With the Whales*. Toronto: McClelland & Stewart, 1989.

Earle, Sylvia A. "Underwater Encounters with Whales." In Wilkes, *Project Interspeak*.

Francis, Daniel. *The Great Chase: A History of World Whaling*. Toronto: Viking, 1990.

Gatenby, Greg, ed. *Whale Sound: An Anthology of Poems About Whales and Dolphins.* Toronto: Dreadnaught, 1977 and Vancouver: J. J. Douglas, 1977.

Gatenby, Greg. *Whales: A Celebration.* Toronto: Prentice-Hall Canada/Lester & Orpen Dennys, 1983.

Graves, Robert. *The Greek Myths.* Harmondsworth, Middlesex, U.K: Penguin, 1960.

Greenwood, Iain. Osprey. www.worldtrans.org/creators/whale/myths.html/.

Hand, Douglas. *Gone Whaling: A Search for Orcas in Northwest Waters.* New York: Simon & Schuster, 1994.

Harkin, Michael. "Whales, Chiefs, and Giants: An Exploration into Nuu-chah-nulth Political Thought," *Ethnology* 1988, 37:4, 317-32.

Heffernan, Thomas Favel. *Stove by a Whale: Owen Chase and the Essex.* Middleton, Conn.: Wesleyan University Press, 1981.

Heyerdahl, Thor. "The Friendly Whale." In Gatenby, *Whales: A Celebration*, 74.

Jacobs, Joseph, ed. *Celtic Fairy Tales.* London: David Nutt, 1892.

Johnson, Terry. "Right to Whale." *Canadian Geographic* 118:1 (Jan/Feb 1988) 37–38.

Kawai, Taeko. "A Vision of the Great Whale." In Gatenby, *Whales: A Celebration*, 153.

Kunz, G. F. *Ivory and the Elephant.* New York: Doubleday, 1916.

Lowenstein, Tom. *Ancient Land: Sacred Whale: The Inuit Hunt and Its Rituals.* New York: Farrar, Straus and Giroux, 1993.

Lucian. *The True History, Book 1.* William Tooke's translation, 1820.

Melville, Herman. *Moby-Dick.* Harmondsworth, Middlesex, U.K.: Penguin, 1972. First published in 1851 as *The Whale.*

McIntyre, Joan. *Mind in the Waters.* New York: Charles Scribner's Sons, 1974.

Nayman, Jacqueline. *Whales, Dolphins, and Man.* London: Hamlyn, 1973.

Nollman, Jim. *The Charged Border: Where Whales and Humans Meet.* New York: Henry Holt, 1999.

Norris, Kenneth S. "Beluga: White Whale of the North." In *National Geographic*, June 1994.

Ommanney, F. D. *Lost Leviathan.* New York: Dodd, Mead. 1971.

O'Meara, John J., trans. *The Voyage of Saint Brendan.* Blackrock, Dublin Co.: Four Courts Press, 1994.

Orbell, Margaret. *The Illustrated Encyclopedia of Maori Myth and Legend.* Christchurch, N.Z.: Canterbury University Press, 1995.

Payne, Roger. *Among Whales.* New York: Charles Scribner's Sons, 1995.

Pliny. *Natural History*, IX, ii, 4. Philemon Holland's translation, 1604.

Rasmussen, K. "The Netselik Eskimos: Social Life and Spiritual Culture." In *Report of the Fifth Thule Expedition, 1921-24*, vol. 8, parts 1-2, 1931.

Reynolds, J. N. "Mocha Dick, or the White Whale of the Pacific." In *The Knickerbocker, New York Monthly Magazine*, XIII (May 1839), 377-92.

Rice, William Hyde. *Hawaiian Legends. Bulletin 29.* Honolulu: Bernice Pauahi Bishop Museum, 1926.

Robertson, R. B. *Of Whales and Men.* New York: Alfred A. Knopf, 1954.

Ross, W. Gillies. *Whaling and Eskimos: Hudson Bay, 1860–1915.* Ottawa: National Museum of Man, 1975.

Rossiter, Bill and Mia. In Wade Doak. *Encounters with Whales and Dolphins.* London: Hodder and Stoughton, 1989.

Sagan, Carl. *The Cosmic Connection.* New York: Doubleday, 1973.

Scammon, Charles Melville. *The Marine Mammals of the Northwestern Coast of North America.* San Francisco: John H. Carmany, 1874. Reprinted New York: Dover, 1968.

Scheffer, Victor B. *The Year of the Whale.* New York: Charles Scribner's, 1969.

Scoresby, William. *Account of the Arctic Regions with a History and Description of the Northern Whale Fishery.* Edinburgh: Archibald Constable, 1820. Reprint Newton Abbot, Devon, U.K.: David & Charles, 1969.

Shuker, Karl. *Dragons: A Natural History.* London: Aurum Press, 1995.

Simpson, Mackinnon, and Robert B. Goodman. *Whale Song: The Story of Hawai'i and the Whale.* n.p.: Beyond Words, n.d.

Skvorecky, Josef. "Bubbles the Whale." In Gatenby, *Whales: A Celebration.*

Small, George. "Why Man Needs the Whales." In Wilkes, *Project Interspeak.*

Strebeigh, Fred. "Hooked on Whales." *Smithsonian* 23:3 (June 1992), 31–41.

Stoett, Peter J. *The International Politics of Whaling.* Vancouver: University of British Columbia Press,

1997.

Swanton, J. R. *Contributions to the Ethnology of the Haida. American Museum of Natural History, Memoirs,* vol. 8, part 1. New York: G. E. Stechert, 1905.

Taylor, Colin, editorial consultant. *Native American Myths and Legends.* London: Salamander, 1994.

Thoreau, Henry David. *The Maine Woods,* Sophia Thoreau and W. E. Channing, eds. Boston: Ticknor and Fields, 1864.

Unterman, Alan. *Dictionary of Jewish Lore and Legend.* London: Thames and Hudson, 1991.

Venables, Bernard. *Baleia! Baleia!* New York: Alfred Knopf, 1969.

Vlessides, Michael. "Licence to Whale." *Canadian Geographic,* 118:1 (Jan/Feb 1998), 24–34.

Wallas, James and Pamela Whitaker. *Kwakiutl Legends As Told to Pamela Whitaker by Chief James Wallas.* North Vancouver and Blaine, Wash.: Hancock House, 1981.

Wilkes, T., ed. *Project Interspeak.* San Francisco: Project Interspeak, 1979.

Williams, Heathcote. *Whale Nation.* London: Jonathan Cape, 1988.

Wilson, Charles. *History of Unilever.* London: Cassell, 1954.

PERMISSIONS

INDEX

ABOUT THE AUTHOR

Jane Billinghurst has been editing natural history titles for the past fifteen years. *The Spirit of the Whale* is her second book. Her first book, *Grey Owl: The Many Faces of Archie Belaney*, was published in 1999. She runs a freelance writing and editorial business in Saskatoon, Saskatchewan, where she lives with her two daughters, Stephanie and Nicola. (Photograph by Gene Hattori, f:11)